THE CAPTIVATED AUDIENCE: HOAXES, ILLUSIONS AND THE BIBLICAL EARTH

THE CAPTIVATED AUDIENCE: HOAXES, ILLUSIONS AND THE BIBLICAL EARTH

PRESSBOOKS.COM

DISCLAIMER

This is a work of non-fiction.

Contents

**Part II. EXPERIMENTS AND
EVIDENCE OF A FLAT EARTH**

Part I

Main Body

I

EPIGRAPH

"In loving memory of our grandparents, Fransisco and Consuelo Delgado."

TABLE OF CONTENTS

———————

———

PREFACE

———

Are you prepared to have your entire world view challenged?

If you are then please proceed with caution, and bring your open mind and your intellect.

This book will explore the dark and nihilistic world that came into fruition by unproven and accepted theories such as gravity, relativity and evolution, to name a few. Just like in the book of Genesis where it explains the generations of Adam, where one person begat another and this person begat that person, the pseudo scientists of the 18th century created one

———

theory that begat another theory and another. This was their means to an end for establishing a mind controlled and conforming society. The secret society succeeded in indoctrinating us all into believing that we are haphazardly flying through the universe being held in place by gravity and relativity from a Big Bang in an ever expanding universe. I am calling this the "Masonic Induced Hypnosis" that we fell under for 500 years now.

The purpose of this book, is to present research and evidence in a way that allows a reader to connect the dots and realize that they have been fooled by a powerful and clandestine secret society. They have made us believe that man created "God," instead of "God" creating man.

So with this short introduction, let us begin.

4

INTRODUCTION

INTRODUCTION

Alexander Ray

My nom de plume is Alexander Ray and I am an ESP Consultant. I have worked as a contractor for ConocoPhillips for over 4 years now, thanks to God. I actually work for a company called Wood Group Production and Consulting. I don't want to bore you too much with my background into my life, and so I will try to keep it short.

I supervise installations of electric submersible pumps (ESPs) into the earth to get oil, and this is called artificial lift. I also trouble shoot electronic variable frequency drives that provides the electronics and logic to speed up and slow down the ESP in order to increase or decrease production. These variable frequency drives send power to a step up transformer, which in turn provides the high voltage that is required, to the downhole motor in order to provide the necessary horse power to do the "work" to lift the oil, water, and gas. This fluid is lifted to surface through impellers and diffusers inside of the electric submersible pumps.

I am intrigued with the different ways that energy transforms, and how we humans have been able to feasibly and prolifically, change the world by extracting fossil fuels in the form of oil from the earth. Once we extract and sell this oil, it gets distributed to the rest of the world as the following: gasoline, natural gas, jet fuel, diesel, and all the derivatives of oil, for example, asphalt, tar, paraffin wax, and lubricating oils.

We use the extracted fossil fuel, to run vehicles, ships, air planes, trains, and even to produce electricity and plastics.

I frequently think about all the physics at work, when all this energy that has been trapped in the earth for millions of years, is converted to other forms of energy including heat energy, mechanical energy, thermal energy, to name a few.

"But did you know that these fuels were once plant and animal life? That's right; fossil fuels are actually the accumulated remains of living organisms that were buried millions of years ago. In fact, it may help you to recall this term by remembering that a 'fossil' is a naturally preserved remnant of a living thing from long ago," says Dr. Rebecca Gillaspy, an instructor at study.com.

Fossil Fuels have trapped energy, theoretically, that came from the sun, and that transferred to these organisms and plants when they were living. It is this energy that is inherent in the fossil fuels, and it is what makes fossil fuels valuable as an energy-rich resource. These ancient organisms have converted to crude oil, coal, natural gas, or heavy oils by exposure to heat and pressure in the earth's crust over hundreds of millions of years.

In my job, I also enjoy trouble shooting and problem solving. Trouble shooting electronic frequency drives, is like solving a big puzzle. My job allows me to use critical thinking every day, in order to visually and mentally solve whatever problem I encounter with the electronic devices that I work with. A friend of mine once said that "you can't fix something unless you know how it works!" I have always found enjoyment in figuring out how things work and why they work, even as a young boy. I remember being fascinated by a Rubik's cube that I bought when it first came out in 1980s. I don't remember ever figuring it out, though, in case you were wondering.

This inquisitive mind of mine, eventually prompted me to investigate the proverbial "rabbit hole" and travel down the path of writing this book today.

I also want to add, that I am a United States Navy Veteran, and I served my country for 6 years from 1989-1995. I have a Kuwait Liberation Medal, which is one of my favorite accolades to date. I was in Operation Desert Shield, Operation Restore Hope and Operation United Shield. I was a boiler technician, Petty Officer 3rd Class in the older steam driven Navy.

My favorite Navy memory is when I became an oil king on the ship. As an oil king, I transferred and tested the ship's fuel oil for bottom sediment and water. Moreover, I was responsible for accounting and tracking all the fuel oil on board the ship including all the potable water, feed water and boiler water. In addition, I tested and maintained boiler water and feed water PH levels and if needed, I injected hydrazine or other chemicals into the boiler feed water. I really enjoyed this job very much and I was only 20 years old when I obtained this prestigious position. I was also in charge of ballasting and de-ballasting the ship when needed as fuel oil was consumed when the ship was underway at sea. The ship's propulsion system and closed loop system that we used back then to provide the energy to move the ship through the water involved many different ways that energy transformed. For example, we used F-76 fuel oil to transfer its energy into the boiler water as superheated steam, and then through auxiliary equipment under pressure, this energy, (now converted to superheated steam), would make its way to the main engines, and turn some big turbines which ultimately turned the ship's propellers through reduction gears. This is how the energy changed from one state to another. The ship's propellers, of course, then pushed the ship through the water.

I just wanted to share this background with you, to establish that I am a very proud and Patriotic American.

I suppose that one of the questions that I have for myself as I write this book, is "Why?"

"Why am I writing this book?"

The main reason, is the following:

I believe that my purpose in life, is to recoup the original belief of the model of the *Earth* as the center of our solar system. In addition, I want to challenge the status quo and together we can speak the truth and bring the necessary change that is warranted.

Another reason in my interest in writing this book, is because sometimes, I lay at night, tossing and turning, pondering about many things about this enigmatic Earth that we live in. I needed a way to express myself and to be able to vent my ideas and thoughts in a creative way.

Ostensibly, I believe that writing my book, offers me this outlet of creativity and inquisition.

I had so many questions, and I needed answers, so I started researching and reading, and taking notes. Furthermore, I visited many websites and watched many videos, and read discussions and blogs in my research. In the end, I learned quite a bit about the Elite or Illuminati, Antarctica, relativity, gravity, space, and about the flat earth. Ultimately, I knew that my goal of writing this book was a genuine and attainable goal.

"It had long since come to my attention that people of accomplishment rarely sat back and let things happen to them. They went out and happened to things."

— Leonardo da Vinci

I want you to know, that I truly and profoundly believe all the life changing ideas and beliefs that I have written in this book.

You only need to look for yourself. Once you question anything that I write here, and you either agree or disagree, then the process of discovery and enlightenment begins.

I will present to you many, "Illusions and Hoaxes," which is part of the book title, by the way, in this book, and I believe that they are fabrications of a powerful secret organization. As to what is their hidden and perverted agenda, is anybody's guess. Some say it is to bring a New World Order.

I choose to believe what Eric Dubay so eloquently says in his *The Flat Earth Conspiracy*, that "By turning Earth into a spinning ball thrown around the Sun and shot through infinite space from a God-less Big Bang they turn humanity into a random meaningless, purposeless accident of a blind, dumb universe! It's trauma-based mind-control! They beat the divinity out of us with their mental manipulations."

The main clandestine agenda of the elite, is the dissemination of "Science," since they act as "Scientific

Dictators" according to Phillip Darrell Collins, for the Academia they created. I will cover this "Scientific Dictators"term in Chapter 3. This theoretical science allowed Freemasons to force their hand on controlling the masses all over the world. What I call the "Evolution Revolution", which occurred in the 17th – 18th century, and continues to this day, was strategically and logistically planned and executed and was achieved during this era.

I will not go into this subject into very much detail, since that may lead my life into a different predicament, altogether, but who knows, it may also lead to another book in the future.

I truly believe in my heart, that I need to share my knowledge with as many people as possible. Furthermore, I would like to add that I am not the first, or the last person to discuss all the subject matter that I will present in my book.

I love the old adage that says, "Aspire to inspire, before you expire."

Therefore, I believe that writing this book is my contribution to society, and that it is one medium that I plan to utilize in order for me to reach as many people as possible. My book is just one small attempt to excite change in our world by making a connection with one person at a time.

Please don't worry, no one will come looking for you by reading this book.

Believe whatever you wish to believe, that is your

prerogative, and that is what is so great about this country that we live in.

Well, unless you discover a crystal ball that can answer all the challenging questions and phenomenon that we will cover in this book, then maybe, a few "Men in Black" might ring your doorbell. "No matter what you do, do not open the door!"

Either way, I hope you open your mind up to this question;

"What if?" "What if, what I am presenting to you in this book is true?"

And if so, then "What else can be possible?"

It is very endearing and special to me, to be embarking on this journey together. After all, reading a book is sort of like taking a journey, wouldn't you agree?

Thank you, for allowing me into your everyday life. (If you indeed, continue reading this book).

Right now, my fiancé is looking at me with trepidation, as I write these lines. She, candidly and not so candidly, has reservations about me writing this book. In addition, she emphatically feels that I will be portrayed in a negative way, or that I will be cast into a stigma as a "quack" or a "conspiracy theorist."

Frankly, I do not care what ignorant people will think.

To continue with this introduction, I would like to share with you all, that I am not an author. But I will try my best to introduce ideas and hypothesis, and explain why I believe in certain observations versus others, as clearly and as articulately as I can.

So, with having said all this, let us delve into the realm of the unknown, and the wacky and the ludicrous. You will soon see that maybe what "You" have been brainwashed to believe, may be the wacky and insane. "Maybe? Maybe not!"

Ultimately, and hopefully, we will start to challenge the status quo!

"What we need is not the will to believe, but the wish to find out."

-William Wordsworth

5

SETTING THE STAGE FOR
THE BOOK

SETTING THE STAGE FOR THE BOOK

Alexander Ray

Leviticus 19:11 (ESV)

"Do not steal." "Do not lie." "Do not deceive one another."

I will also quote from the Bible in this book. It is the ultimate authoritative word that showed me the truth about the Earth that we live in.

"I strongly believe, that the Earth is Flat." "There I said it."

My statement that the "Earth is Flat", sets the stage for the theme of this book.

I will show you a picture of what I mean.

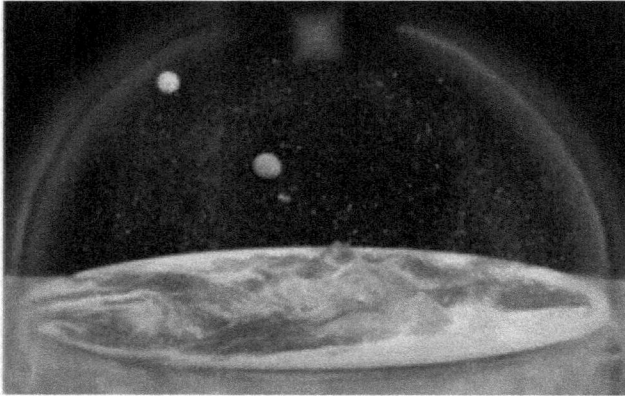

I will be challenging and presenting many controversial theories, ideas and sanctified truths that are the very fabric of our world and its existence.

I am just one of the many people in the world that refuses to believe without empirical proof. To determine what is real and what isn't real, I use my 5 senses, and I also use my God given common sense among other things; along with my education, life experiences and my willingness to investigate. Lastly, I use my 6th sense of intuition.

I know what you might be asking yourself now. If I said

that I do not believe certain phenomenon, then why, for example, do I believe in God the Almighty as our creator?

I will tell you why in this book, if you continue reading.

Psalms 118:8 (KJV) "It is better to trust in the Lord than to put confidence in man."

Yes, please look around you and ponder "What is reality?"

Is it like the Matrix, the movie?

I am just kidding, this isn't that kind of book. "Well maybe....just maybe."

In writing my book, I will also use many quotes from many famous dead people. The following is an example of what I mean:

"I think therefore I am."

-Rene Descartes

The meaning of these few words are profound and I believe this means that we, as divine human beings created by God, have the ability to be aware of "oneself." This sets "us" humans apart as individuals which distinguishes us from any other species on this planet. We are endowed with certain abilities that no other animal on this planet possesses, and that is the ability to speak and write. Therefore, we can share information to each other and allow access for generations by passing it down through books, newspapers, magazines, documents, notes, internet articles, etc. This allows the human race to learn and prosper albeit, sometimes we enslave ourselves by propagating lies and deceit.

Another deliberate quote that I am going to borrow for this book is the following:

"If you would be a real seeker after truth, it is necessary that at least once in your life you doubt, as far as possible, all things."

— Rene Descartes

Just as a side note, many of the intellectual discoveries, and beliefs that I have come to accept have happened to me within the last year (2015). I am a newbie when it comes to the Flat Earth truth.

I want to share this with you because when I accepted these truths, I would have loved to have stumbled across and found a book that contained all of the different topics that I am going to write about. I have already done the research and I hope it is easy to follow along.

This is the reason for all the different topics in all the chapters of my book. I wanted to scratch the surface, so to speak, on certain intriguing topics in that particular chapter. However, please realize, that the topic in that chapter, is intertwined and germane to the completeness of the "big picture" that I am trying to articulate with words. In layman's terms, one topic helps explain another and another and so forth until you get to the end of the book. Once you follow all the proverbial bread crumbs you will decide for yourself which deception or hoax will spark enough curiosity in you to make you see the world from a different perspective.

Once you accept that NASA lies to us all, and that science is a powerful tool that keeps us in check, you will be able to connect the dots for yourself.

"If" you do accept my book as a possibility, I wish to ask you to pay it forward, and inform someone else about my book so they can enjoy it.

Once again, I hope that my book can be your guide into this new paradigm shift, and I also dream that this book becomes a valuable resource for you.

There is a plethora of wonderful books, documentaries, videos and reading material for you to enjoy once you decide to become one of us Flat Earth proponents.

Maybe, you will not accept that the earth is flat, but you may instead, believe and pursue interests in some of the other topics in my chapters. Whatever, final outcome your journey may have, you can become influential to the future of this world that we live in.

Please realize that, "You is kind, you is smart, you is important."

— Kathryn Stockett, The Help

This is a quote from a famous movie that we watch over and over at home, by the way.

"If" the Earth is indeed "Flat", then, I accept and believe that we also live inside of a dome or a firmament. They go hand in hand, the flat earth and the firmament, that is.

Without this firmament, life on Earth could not exist. I read this somewhere and I profoundly believe this truth.

I know that this is another major concept to introduce, and it is hard to even fathom.

But if you bear with me, I will indulge and entertain your brain.

"What?" "Do we live in a snow globe?" "It sounds totally ridiculous!" "Right?"

But wait, please let me defend my statements before I lose you here.

I know that there are people that believe in the legendary Bigfoot, but to me, that is simply absurd.

Let me elucidate:

The footprints that were found that sparked the legend of Bigfoot, turned out to be from a big bear, since when bears walk on all fours, sometimes they step on the same print twice when they cross walk. Bears also stand on their hind legs and walk that way and if seen at night or from a distance, could be mistaken for something else.

There is a documentary where I saw a bear expert recreate the exact Bigfoot print after he had a bear walk across mud they had laid as a path using dirt and water, and then the bear expert cast a mold of the bear paw prints. Once the mold dried it looked eerily familiar to the Bigfoot footprints.

Just so you know, a normal bear paw print does get elongated as the bear steps on the front paw print with its hind legs.

Regardless of hard evidence, many people and enthusiasts choose to believe the Big Foot legend.

For example, for several years, many Bigfoot followers were certain that a few hair samples that they had, came from the legendary monster. "More than half of the 30 samples that underwent DNA analysis were linked to sightings of Bigfoot in the United States, ranging from Texas and Minnesota to Arizona and Washington State," according to an article entitled "Bigfoot, Yeti and beyond."

However, after sending off the samples to a lab, the DNA was matched to "black bears, cows, a porcupine, horse, raccoon, sheep, dear, canines," according to the same article from Nbcnews.com.

In "Yeti, Big Foot debunked: DNA reveals the bear facts," from yahoo.com it reiterated the following: "The 18 "Big Foot" samples were found to have a wide range of real world sources, ranging from the American black bear, raccoon and cow to a porcupine and either a wolf, coyote or dog." Two of the Yeti samples matched up to animals like a polar bear, goat like animal, and a Malaysian Tapir. Bryan Sykes is the man that spearheaded this yearlong effort to gather all the DNA. He is a genetics professor from Oxford University.

In describing how the legend of Bigfoot was born or made, let me try to briefly capture some of the chronological events that occurred in the past 50-60 years.

Bob Titmus was one of the first persons to sell the first casts of the giant mysterious print which he found around Bluff Creek, in California, in 1958 and 1959.

When the mold was cast, "Voila!" instant monster and legend was born.

Then you get a guy in a very convincing hominid-like creature, Sasquatch suit and a shaky camera and the very famous video spreads like wildfire. I am of course, talking about the Patterson film of 1967.

But to deflate this legend, there was a man named Bob Heironimus, who stated that he was the man that donned the costume for the famous Roger Patterson film in 1967. He even took a lie detector and passed.

You can find this on YouTube from unexplainedmonsters, and it is entitled "Lie detector of Bob "Bigfoot" Heironimus-Man in the suit." It is actually from a show called "Lie Detector" and the host is a woman named, Rolanda Watts.

Bob states that "the video was a flagrant hoax in order for the men involved in faking the video to make money." Bob added that he was supposed to get paid 1000 dollars, but that never happened. He wanted to clear his conscience and come clean and that is why he wanted to tell the world that the film was a hoax.

This brief tangent to the legendary hairy beast, is what most of this book will deal with, hoaxes and other interesting topics. If you noticed, I presented evidence that clarifies and debunks that legend of Bigfoot.

Moreover, if you notice, no real DNA or skeleton of the giant primate has ever been found buried. Looks like the only thing buried now is the legend of Bigfoot.

Sometimes people, even when presented with facts, choose to believe in fantasies and hoaxes.

"There are two ways to be fooled. One is to believe what isn't true; the other is to refuse to believe what is true."

-Soren Kierkegaard

Returning to the original subject of this chapter, of what people believe, some people on Earth, believe in aliens from outer space.

Aliens on Earth? How is this even possible?

I do not believe that this is possible, since the Firmament forms an unbreachable glass dome or wall. (I will cover this subject in chapter 7.)

So much for the Roswell crash landings and the alien body that was supposedly found. The Air Force has reported that the supposed alien bodies were nothing more than "anthropomorphic test dummies that were carried aloft by high altitude balloons for scientific research." I obtained this information from James McAndrews' *The Roswell Report: Case Closed.*

Then, there are people that believe NASA's trips to the moon as authentic, and that humans have landed on the moon.

This is a very "controversial" subject, however, I included this in the book, as well. Once I present undeniable evidence of fakery from NASA, you may agree that everything starts to make more sense. The lies that come from the Illuminati and Freemasons are like an onion. The more you peel the more layers there are.

Like I said before, I will aim to arouse your intellectual stimulation. The more you read, the more this will happen.

Some people believe that we have sent space crafts to Mars, and other planets, even to the Sun to study it.

Really?

Still others genuinely believe that the New Horizons space craft was launched in 2006 and did a Pluto flyby in 2015 and then it sent real pictures of Pluto back to Earth.

As you can see, in the released NASA image below, you can actually see what looks like the Disney character Pluto's face outline on the bottom right face of the planet! I know you may think I manipulated this picture of the dwarf planet Pluto, but I assure I have not.

NASA and the Illuminati are probably laughing so hard at the stuff that they get away with in presenting fake photographs and composite drawings, and disseminating this data as real. A picture of Pluto on the planet's face? If this doesn't "rattle your chain" or get "you riled up", I don't know what will.

NASA and the Illuminati mock God, and so mocking us, is fun and games. But don't worry, my job is to help you see the deceptions.

I know, that maybe you are wondering about everything that you have just read.

As I have previously mentioned, it took me a long while to accept all the improbabilities, however, slowly but surely, I began to notice the fake NASA deceptions.

I too, was once part of the "Captivated Audience."

However, once I stumbled upon what seems like a bunch of lies that come from NASA, everything concerned with space became open to speculation. I mean pictures and images that have been photo shopped and doctored, should be scrutinized and questioned when NASA presents them as real.

I was in your shoes, once, and I had **No** reason whatsoever, to question anything that ever came from NASA concerning space and the universe.

My entire life, I had been taught in school that the earth is a spinning globe and that gravity is the force that holds everything together.

"Right?" "Of course it is."

Well, I hope if anything, that this book will, at the very least, fascinate you, and at most, possibly even persuade you to continue to explore and question everything that you see around you.

Finally, I hope that you are ready to begin the exciting journey into exploring all the reasons why I believe that the earth is flat among many other revelations.

In corroboration with this statement, there will be many theories and models that will be explored, and challenged and then either supported or debunked.

To reiterate, this entire book, will be dealing with various theories, statements, ideas, and personal opinions. Some have been proven to be true, in articles and videos and websites and some facts are considered part of our history.

Other ideas and theories are speculations and personal

conclusions. Some have been challenged for many years, even centuries.

However, like any intelligent human being, you should ultimately, do your own research and make your own observations and assumptions and draw your own conclusions.

Hopefully, this book will be your first step in a long journey into that direction.

I almost forgot to mention, that hopefully, some bona fide Flat Earth authors, also read this book and enjoy it. Maybe, we can share resources one day, and I can continue to grow mentally, spiritually and fundamentally in my knowledge of the Flat Earth and why the earth is not a spinning ball.

Ultimately, I hope that every reader, regardless of your country, race, religion, or upbringing, can find your own "Aha moment!" and I hope you also find something worth remembering about my book.

I do not know "how", or even "if", my life will change by writing this book. But, I am very excited to finally begin the arduous and daunting task of writing this book.

My inspiration is our Lord Jesus Christ, my beautiful wife, and our kids, and our doggie Neeko.

I also have a sister that is a published author, and whom I respect and admire dearly.

I will be turning to her for help in navigating the waters of getting published, once my book is complete, God willing.

She encouraged me to take the leap of faith, of writing and I hope you enjoy this book.

So now, let me ask you,

"What do you believe?"

6

MOON LANDING OF 1969

Moon Landing of 1969

Just to give you a little bit of history into how my "belief transformation", happened, I'd like to give you more insight into my "Aha moment!"

"Do you remember the statement that I made earlier, about people that believe that humans landed on the moon?"

There is an astounding percentage of the population of the world that believes that American astronauts went to the moon 6 different times in the late 1960's to early 1970's. I am not one of those believers.

So that makes me the kind of person that believes that

NASA pulled perhaps the biggest hoax of all time!

Will they ever come clean? Probably never!

I mean they swindled billions of dollars from the hard working tax payers in the United States of America for the exuberant space program.

I think now is the opportune time for a quote from Revelations.

Revelations 22:15 (ESV)

"Outside are the dogs and sorcerers and the sexually immoral and murderers and idolaters, and everyone who loves and practices falsehood."

Herein, lies the second part of my book's title that deals with "Hoaxes, and Illusions."

I wish it was true about the moon landing, I mean, it would have truly been, one of the most monumental achievements of mankind.

"If", only it were true. The only way that I saw the light, so to speak, was by having an open mind.

Fortunately for me, my "Aha moment" happened, and everything about NASA started to unravel in front of my eyes.

And so, this is how it happened:

One fateful evening at home, while I was on my IPad watching videos on YouTube, I stumbled upon a video entitled "A Funny Thing Happened on the way to the Moon." This video, undoubtedly was my "Aha Moment!"

It is a 2001 film written, produced and directed by Bart Sibrel, and it is an absolutely astonishing film.

And after watching the film, I can honestly say that, this film unequivocally changed my life.

At this exact moment, during watching this video, I felt like I was punched in the stomach, but I did not know why I felt this way. I felt like I couldn't catch my breath. More than anything, I felt betrayed.

Why, you ask, did I feel this way?

Well, if you watch the same video, you will see for yourself.

I was looking at video evidence of our three revered astronauts, Neil Armstrong, Buzz Aldrin and Michael Collins and that they were half way to the moon.

In the film, Neil Armstrong, a Freemason by the way, stated that they were some 130,000 miles away from Earth (halfway to the Moon) when they were actually only in low earth orbit. You can actually see the white clouds of earth outside of their window when the video camera is pointed in that direction.

In the scene that I am describing, Neil Armstrong actually says to NASA main control that they were half way to the moon. In reality, the astronauts were filming out of the space craft's small round window and they held a cut out circular crescent shape that made the earth look small. Furthermore, since the window was round shape, it helped "sell" (to the people of the world that was going to be watching) the idea that the earth is round/sphere shape. Ingeniously, they achieved a very duplicitous (deceitful) shot, but interestingly enough, it did look very convincing, as if they really were far, far away from earth.

A third party, which many have stated was the CIA, is heard giving instructions to Neil Armstrong on when to speak. The person on the other line of the phone call actually tells Neil Armstrong "TALK", when main control in Houston, Texas tried to hail Neil Armstrong on the radio, about a question.

They wanted to fool the live broadcast audience by counting the few seconds of time delay in order to fake that they were indeed far away, and since if they really were heading to the moon, the transmission of the voice signals would take a few seconds to get back. The third party was in charge of counting the few seconds time and then coaching Neil of when to "Talk."

In addition, the video as well as the audio that the astronauts had previously prepared with this fake shot, at that moment, was actually broadcasted at a later time and presented to the world as "live." However, they were in essence rehearsing a play.

Of course, the historical aired "fake footage" gave a glimpse of a tiny earth, thanks to the "illusion" that they had already perfected, and people had no reason to doubt if the astronauts were flying to the moon like NASA and the video showed.

One thing that I do want to point out about the televised footage of the actual famous moon walk by Neil Armstrong is, "Why were TV stations only allowed to broadcast in black and white and off of a silver screen?"

The "Captivated Audience" was actually watching a copy
of a copy. It was meticulously planned out this way so that
any mistakes in the studio where they were filming the
actual moon landing would not be easily noticeable.

The proverbial, "nail in the coffin", about the Moon
landing being a hoax, was that the date of this film, that
was given to Mr. Sibrel, (and which was not intended for
public broadcast) was presented with the exact same 3 days
that the Apollo astronauts were supposedly heading to the
moon and landing on the moon.

This is ludicrous, since on July 20th 1969, the date when
Neil Armstrong supposedly had a date with

"history", and set foot on the surface of the moon. They
were still in the command module manipulating the inside
of the space craft lighting to make it dark to simulate the
darkness of space, and then shooting the earth by making
it look small from out the round window of the space
command module with the prepared crescent shaped cutout. The crescent shape, just in case you didn't know, was
to make the imprint of the terminator line around the
earth which separates night and day; that is if you
subscribe to the earth being a globe shape.

In the same scene, Neil Armstrong, was pointing the
camera towards the small window, and telling the
"Captivated Audience" that the camera they were using
was actually up against the edge of the window and
capturing the panoramic view of the tiny earth since they
were so far away. Unfortunately for them, we see Michael

Collins or Buzz Aldrin accidentally exposes his arm across the shot of the small earth, and you can see the hairs of his arm. How can this be possible? In other words, let us just pretend for a minute that they were indeed 130,000 miles away from earth. How could we see a hairy arm come in between the camera and the window since they stated that the camera was pressed against the window? How?

Then, Neil Armstrong frantically tries to pan away and zoom out, since he panics when he sees this. Just to reiterate, however, the film was unedited footage. It gave NASA plenty of time to manipulate the film and delete this scene for the "live" broadcasting.

In the film, once Michael Collins removes the cutout crescent shape from the window, we can clearly see the sun light come in through the window and we can clearly view the blue and white clouds of the earth sky from outside and the low earth orbit altitude where they were the entire time during filming. Also, this video footage was in color. However, NASA stated that they did not have a color camera with them on the trip to the moon.

Like magicians, NASA and the astronauts were setting up an "illusion," which is how magic tricks are conducted and orchestrated, and the more attention to detail, the more believable and wonderful the illusion becomes once it is executed to a "Tee." I'd like to add that "the devil really is in the details"

One time, we saw magician Criss Angel, turn himself into a small autonomous 3 foot tall dummy sitting on a chair on the stage, and then he appeared inside of a larger mechanical robot, on stage at one of his magic shows in Las

Vegas. How did he do this? It looked so real to me, and I could not see any obvious explanation. The difference between this illusion, and NASA's illusion, is that in Vegas, "The Captivated Audience," exclusively surrenders their beliefs to the magician, in order to be entertained. However, the illusion that NASA perpetrated on mankind was deception.

I personally think that this tiny fake picture of Earth is used in many photographs as part of NASA's propaganda, and although disingenuous, it looks real.

This unedited video of the astronauts engaging in a not-so-clandestine operation to fool the world, was the "Smoking Gun" proof about humans not landing on the moon. As a result of this film, it made me acquire a "no stone unturned" kind of mentality, and I was consumed to find the truth. This subject about the moon landing is controversial and people do not like to be questioned about it. I know that in another Bart Sibrel video entitled "Astronauts Gone Wild," that the astronauts sure as heck didn't appreciate all the inflammatory questions about the Lunar landing!

Now that you have been presented with some evidence about the lunar landing hoax, maybe you will be interested

in further researching this outlandish and meticulous

hoax that was pulled on the entire world.

In the words of the hip song by Red Hot Chili Peppers "Californication", "Space may be the final frontier but it's made in a Hollywood basement."

There is a great book written, by Bill Kaysing and Randy Reid entitled "We Never Went to the Moon," and I highly recommend it. It presents countless evidence of forgery and raises questions concerning the Apollo missions to the moon.

Another great book that I recommend, is a book written by Ralph Rene, entitled "NASA Mooned America!" You can imagine what that book is about!

Still there is about as many books that try to debunk the hoax theorists as there are about the moon landing being a real historical fact. I want to say that after many months of research, I have concluded, without a shadow of a doubt, or without a shadow of the earth, that we did not go to the moon, and that no human being ever will!

The moon landing hoax, really was the very first thing, that got my wheels turning, so to speak, and it made me question all that I have ever been taught in school about space, earth and black holes, satellites, the International Space Station, and many other things.

It's like removing a blindfold, it really is, and the vision that you have once it is removed is high-definition and crystal clear.

Speaking of crystal clear vision, there is an expert that I think is very instrumental in exposing NASA as big illusionists. His name is David Percy and he spent countless hours examining genuine photographs of the Apollo missions. He is a photo expert and award winning cinematographer and a whistle blower.

He directed a film entitled "What Happened on the Moon?" It is an investigation into Apollo, and it was made in 2000.

Mr. Percy has found many anomalies and discrepancies in the photos. He contends that the shadows cast by objects from the Apollo photos should be going in only one direction.

The basic gist of it is this: In space, there should only be light source, which is the sun.

Therefore, Percy says that the angle of the shadows as they hit certain objects, like the flag on the moon and the LEM, (Lunar Extraction Module) should line up and fall in the same direction. But the shadows don't. Also, the length of the shadows from the same objects should be the same length and not different lengths.

One of the big problems that I had believing the entire fabulous ordeal of the astronauts landing on the moon, was how pristine and grandiose the photos are. However, the camera that the astronauts used was a cumbersome Hasselblad 500 EL data camera.

It was mounted to the astronaut's chest area and that is how they took all the pictures. A person has to wonder, if the astronauts had big gloves on their hands, then how could they manage such nice photographs?

There was an experiment that I read about in an article from aplanetruth.info called, #12 How Did Apollo Moonwalkers Survive 200 F + Temps. They placed these same style astronaut gloves under a vacuum and "experiments prove absolutely that such gloves are impossible to use and that the wearer cannot bend the wrist or fingers to do any dexterous work whatsoever when filled with 5 psi over ambient pressure either in a vacuum or in the earth's atmosphere."

Therefore it's dubious to me, of how the astronauts were able to manipulate their hands and fingers and press a button repeatedly and take such great photographs on their supposed moon excursion, if they were in the vacuum of space. The pressure inside the space suit was to avoid anything from the outside to penetrate their suits.

I read that the astronauts practiced with the camera, 24/7, so that they could become experts here on earth, before their trip to the moon. But, the beautiful pictures from the moon that they took, makes me wonder their authenticity. For example, the cross hairs that are supposed to be centered in every picture from the Hasselblad camera film, is another concern. But the crosshairs don't always show up where they should in the photographs. Sometimes the crosshairs appear behind objects when they are supposed to be in front of these objects. The crosshairs should never be behind on a photo, and by this deductive reasoning, if it does appear behind any object, then the photo has been altered or cropped.

In The Apollo Moon Landing Hoax: Proof Positive that the Recent LRO Images of the 'Apollo Landing Sites' Were Photoshopped Fakes!' Northernseeker explains that "just a few years back, the Lunar Reconnaissance Orbiter (LRO), that was at the time circling the moon, was directed by operators at the NASA Jet Propulsion Laboratory to take

some pictures of the supposed Apollo landing sites. That was done after years of everyone saying that they wanted positive proof that men actually walked on the moon by having the actual landing sites photographed from either on Earth, or from lunar orbit."

This pictures were taken back in February of 2012.

However, after some delay from NASA to provide the photographs, experts indicated that the photos clearly appeared to have been manipulated, according to Hunchbacked's evidence of fraud of the LRO images. You can check the video out yourself on YouTube: under "The Proof that the LRO Photos are Photoshopped."

Still one of my favorite websites concerning all the photo manipulations by NASA is the following:

www.atlanteanconspiracy.com

This is the website of my hero, and Flat Earth Research President Eric Dubay.

Please look at all the photographs and the brief explanations for each photograph, by reading the descriptions and you will start to notice how NASA manipulates the photography in order to make people believe that we went to the moon. I wanted to include some of the pictures here, but there are just too many to make it feasible for this book.

For example, you will find tracks on the surface of the moon from the lunar rover, when the rover hasn't even been deployed yet.

Also, why isn't there a speck of dust on the landing pads of the Lunar Extraction Module? The thrust from any rocket engine, even a small one on the LEM, as it descended onto the lunar surface would have displaced a ton of dirt and surely would have covered some of the landing pads. When I work out in the oilfield and we get bad dust storms here in Odessa, Texas, I have to hurry up and shut the door to my pickup truck, lest I get dirt all up inside my truck interior.

I can't imagine how much dust would be blowing by the powerful rocket engine of the LEM thrusting down to land on the lunar surface and blowing the fine dust powder everywhere. Surely, a speck of dust would have made it into one of the photos that were taken.

While we are on the subject of the LEM, I want to include this quick note about the LEM. Neil Armstrong couldn't even land the LEM in earth's atmosphere. There are videos where you will see what I am referring to here.

When Mr. Armstrong flew the prototype LEM, on earth, he had to eject right before the LEM crash landed to earth, to save his life. Yet we are supposed to believe that he mastered the controls in a 1/4 of the earth's gravity and landed it on the moon, with a far less complex computer than a pocket calculator from the 1980's, or your cell phone for that matter.

More fakery is clearly visible in photos of Buzz Aldrin when you pay attention to the gloves he is wearing. In some photos he is wearing black gloves, and in other photos, he is wearing gray gloves?

This would be quite a daunting task since the astronaut's suit is pressurized and changing gloves at random would not make any sense. Buzz Aldrin would have to pressurize and depressurize to change gloves right? That would mean he would have to climb back onboard the lunar module to change gloves and then back out to be photographed by Neil Armstrong who is the one that took all the photographs with the chest mounted camera.

Speaking of cameras mounted on their chest area, I found the following informative article entitled "Did We

Land on the Moon? A Debunking of the Moon Hoax Theory." It says that "if Neil Armstrong was the first man on the Moon, then who shot the video of him descending the ladder and taking his initial steps on the lunar surface." The article of course goes on to defend this observation by saying that there was some kind of lanyard that Armstrong pulled where the camera rested on a pallet at the foot of the LEM and then Aldrin switched the camera on to capture the historic video. Seems like NASA has an answer or explanation for everything.

Another major concern about the improbability of

humans on the moon, is the intense temperature swing on the moon and the hostile environment there.

The temperature of the moon is said to range from 253 degrees Fahrenheit in the day due to the immense heat from the sun, to -243 degrees Fahrenheit at night, according to Tim Sharp from space.com, and this hostile environment would have definitely affected the film in the camera.

How could the film survive this harsh environment?

There is also the Van Allen Radiation Belts, which are intense radiation belts that surround the earth and which would have fried the film on its way to the moon and back. (I will cover the Van Allen belts more in another chapter). It would have probably fried humans also, by the way.

In an outstanding website https://aplanetruth.info, I found an article entitled #12 How Did Apollo Moonwalkers Survive 200 F + Temps?

This website talks about the spacesuits and temperature and the lack of any plausible explanation from NASA as to how the space suits were cooled. Truthseeker goes on his soap box and proclaims:

"An air conditioner cannot, and will not work without a heat exchanger. A heat exchanger simply takes heat gathered in a medium such as Freon from one place and transfers it to another place. This requires a medium of molecules which can absorb and transfer the heat such as an atmosphere or water. An air conditioner will not and cannot work in a vacuum. A space suit surrounded by a vacuum cannot transfer heat from the inside of the suit to any other place. The vacuum, remember, is a perfect insulator. A man would roast in his suit in such a circumstance.

"NASA claims the spacesuits were cooled by a water system which was piped around the body, then through a system of coils sheltered from the sun in the backpack. NASA claims that water was sprayed on the coils causing a coating of ice to form. The ice then supposedly absorbed the tremendous heat collected in the water and evaporated into space. There are two problems with this that cannot be explained away. 1.) The amount of water needed to be carried by the astronauts in order to make this work for even a very small length of time in the direct 55 degrees over the boiling point of water (210 degrees F at sea level on Earth) heat of the sun could not have possibly been carried by the astronauts. 2.) NASA has since claimed that they found ice in moon craters. NASA claims that ice sheltered from the direct rays of the sun will NOT evaporate destroying their own bogus "air conditioning" explanation."

In my research, I did find that the LEM did have some kind of a/c system, according to NASA, that supposedly ran only on batteries.

What kind of batteries could pull this off, I'd like to know. (I dedicate this section, to my brother-in- law from North Carolina. He is a very astute air conditioning technician from North Carolina. One time we were having a discussion about this very section in my book. He and my sister were visiting for my wedding back in April).

However, quoting from the previous website, "NASA knows (better than to claim, in addition, that a water cooling apparatus such as that which they claim cooled the astronaut suits cooled the spacecraft. No rocket could ever have been launched with the amount of water needed to work such a system for even a very short period of time. Fresh water weighs a little over 62 lbs. per cubic foot. Space and weight capacity were critical given the lift capability of the rockets used in the Apollo Space Program. No such extra water was carried by any mission whatsoever for Suits, or for cooling the spacecraft."

There is still so much more information and websites and videos that propose the moon landings as being a hoax. I would have to devote an entire book to only this one topic, however, I wanted to touch on the main points that seem to indicate than NASA lied to us all.

One major question that the die-hard believers use is "How was the Apollo moon landing a hoax, if everyone saw the rocket launch the astronauts into space on July 16th, 1969?"

As I have heard it explained in my research is that the rocket did launch from Cape Kennedy Florida from launch pad 39A. However, it probably landed somewhere in the Pacific Ocean after the craft was out of sight and out of mind. If you Google rocket launches or the space shuttle launches, you will notice that they always launch near an ocean.

In other words, pay attention as to why rockets always take a weird trajectory when they launch. As they go up, eventually they turn at almost a 90 degree turn. These powerful energy thrusting fuel consumption vehicles, do not launch straight into space. Even when rockets are being tested, they seem to turn instead of going straight up. I think that the answer is because of the unbreachable firmament that they will encounter.

Please do a search on the internet for videos involving rocket launches. There is never a continuous video that is shot where the rocket launches and reaches space and orbits the earth or doing any kind of space travel.

Experts have speculated that rockets cannot breach the biblical firmament which is up in space. Therefore, there are no such thing as ICBM, or intercontinental ballistic missiles.

One main example, that I would like to mention to help prove my point is the following:

In the very dangerous Cuban Missile crisis of 1962 between the U.S. and the Soviet Union some missiles had been placed in Cuba and, the extreme close proximity between Cuba and Florida was something very worrisome. 90 miles is the distance between Cuba and Florida and a missile could easily reach this range, and this fact posed a serious threat to American lives. The infamous Cuban Missile Crisis was a 13 day intense chess match that President John F. Kennedy and Nikita Khrushchev played with nuclear warheads. Thank God, they carefully averted a World War.

Notwithstanding this Armageddon scenario, ICBMs were not the real issue during this crisis.

Why not?

ICBMs cannot breach the firmament and go into space and then travel through space from one continent to another.

Therefore, we should not have to lose sleep and stress out about North Korea, or countries that are far away. It is merely propaganda to instill fear and peddle whatever propaganda the Illuminati are plotting.

However, I digress with this information.

Where were we, oh yes, we were discussing the Apollo rocket launch with astronauts onboard. When the astronauts go "up in space" they are really only in low earth orbit and since "what goes up must come down" they have to return to land on earth. The reentry vehicle is then probably carried and dropped by a cargo plane and then the parachutes are deployed on the capsule as it lands in the ocean. I watched a video interview with Bill Kaysing and Bob Sibrel, (another 2 of my heroes) and Bill told a story of an airline pilot who shared that he and his copilot had seen a cargo airplane drop a command module one time, when they were on a flight to Japan, and they could see the trajectory of the free falling capsule up until the point when the parachutes deployed as it reached the ocean. They were astonished, but it makes sense.

The news media coverage always conveniently shows the astronauts emerging from the capsule after they land in the ocean.

Bill Kaysing, a moon hoax investigator, brought up many devastating observations to deflate the NASA hoax of flying to the moon. He worked at Rocketdyne, and he was involved with the rocket engines and the different propellants used for the supposed Apollo missions. After witnessing all the shady and subpar contractors that set the low standard for NASA's space program, and researching the disaster prone rockets and incidents during the space age, Mr. Kaysing decided to write a book and to become a moon hoax investigator. He honestly did not think that they could get to the moon with the technology of the time, hence his belief that the Moon landing was a hoax, when he saw it televised.

Another keen observation that I wanted to share, is why don't we ever see steam flashing and engulfing the re-entry vehicle when it touches down in the ocean? Bill Kaysing says that when the command module enters the earth's atmosphere, it generates a lot of friction due to the high speed and the friction through the molecules in the atmosphere, making the bottom extremely hot, like 4 digit degree Fahrenheit hot, and so when this blazing hot surface touches the 50 or 60 degree Fahrenheit ocean water, we should see instant flashes of steam erupting from the ocean. However, in all the footage of any landing of the module, we never see this. I mean if the temperature of the metal is at least one thousand degrees Fahrenheit when it touches the much cooler ocean water, we should see instant flash steam erupting instantly.

Remember my opening introduction about physics and how energy changes? Water has 3 different states and will change depending on its temperature and pressure. Since the water that is touching the metal is the cooling medium in direct contact with this extremely hot temperature the initial temperature differential should cause this phenomenon.

Another explanation that I have also heard is that the astronauts were never onboard the Saturn V rocket during the first Apollo mission to the moon. In other words, they entered and exited the rocket, so not to endanger their lives. Then the rocket is shown to launch, and once the vantage point where the camera that is fixated on the rocket is reached and the rocket seems to disappear, nobody questions if the rocket is in space or fell to the ocean.

I want to continue giving more reasons into all the various clues and evidence that lead me to doubt that we ever went to the moon.

What I want to do now, is shift gears to the relevant present day and current NASA projects.

Please look up a video on YouTube entitled NASA Engineer Kelly Smith admits they can't get past the Van Allen Belts.

In this video, they talk about how NASA is exploring and

testing the atmosphere, space, and radiation in order to one day, be able to send humans to the Moon.

Wait what? I thought we already went in 1969? We ended up going to the moon, not once but 6 times. That is a total of 12 times that the astronauts passed through the lethal radiation belts and went to the Moon without any accidents or deaths.

Smith ascertains the presence and devastating phenomenon know at the Van Allen belts that he says is a radiation death trap.

Smith says and I quote, "Radiation like this could harm the guidance systems, onboard computers, or other electronics on Orion." Smith continues saying that "shielding will be put to the test, as the vehicle cuts through the waves of radiation."

"Then scientists will analyze all the data collected from all the different types of sensors that are onboard Orion. They will study this data and understand it completely before they send humans through this region in space."

I got all this information from the same video "NASA Engineer admits they can't get past the Van Allen Belts."

What did he just say? They can't get past the Van Allen Belts? So how did we send humans to the Moon in 1969?

Yes, please, look up the video, and hopefully NASA won't erase it by then.

Bart Sibrel asked for the readings of the Orion spacecraft's onboard Geiger Counters in REM, from NASA but they gave him the run around, and told him it was top secret. He would have to file paperwork to the NSA or something like that, and he shared this information in "Crappy Anniversary: Did We Walk on the Moon 46 Years Ago with 1960's Technology?"

I just recently found out that in the days when NASA was experimenting with sending living breathing organisms into space, they sent a total of 32 monkeys into space in order to test the effect of space travel.

The very first monkey was named Albert and he died on a V2 rocket that went up 39 miles. However, this monkey died of suffocation. The next monkey, appropriately named Albert II, did survive the flight and went up 83 miles, which is considered space, according to Wikipedia.

I wish to give credit where credit is due here. I do believe that NASA and other space agencies may have valiantly and honorably tried their very best to go into space. However, the true reality of the restrictions and the grand master plan from our Creator, does not permit this. There is a limit and boundary of where we can travel on this earth.

For example, the deepest humans have ever drilled or dug is about 7 miles or 35,000 feet. However, they have a hypothesis of what the earth's core looks like and its physical and chemical properties. The highest a human has ever been is about 400 miles but I even doubt that height.

So back to the Moon hoax, since I digress.

I had seen an episode on MythBusters where they actually appeared to debunk the moon hoax theorists. At that time, I actually started to believe once again that maybe the U.S. did send 3 astronauts to the moon in 1969.

However, if you look up "Prepare to be Busted" a video by Jarrah White, he shows that the MythBusters botched the experiment where they tried to simulate the same 1/6th gravity on the moon walk, hops and skips that the astronauts use.

In the video, this exact weightless walk can be achieved by using a gravity rig, plus by then slowing the video by 67%. When you do this, you get the exact height and motion as the supposed astronauts on the moon. Exact match!

The MythBusters obviously muffed the experiments by using one experiment at a time instead of together. Yes, they were so close, or maybe, they weren't allowed to show both experiments simultaneously since this would have replicated the exact moon walk motion of the astronauts.

Part of NASA's agenda was and continues to be to propagate whatever lies to indoctrinate humans to believe that the earth is a perfect ball.

For example, one of the experiments that the astronauts did when they were on the Moon, was dropping a hammer and a feather, and according to them, it was to prove that Galileo was right about falling objects in gravity fields. David Scott was the astronaut who did the experiment on Apollo 15 mission.

You can find videos disproving this experiment by

dropping a feather and a hammer here on earth and manipulating the film speed.

There is a video on YouTube, where on the same Apollo mission, there is the sound of hammer impact as an astronaut hits a pole that he is trying to drive into the lunar surface.

How can this be heard, if there is no atmosphere on the moon and thus no sound waves to carry the vibrations that the hammer would make as it hit the pole? This is kind of like when someone asks you, "If a tree falls in a forest, and no one is around to hear it, does it make a sound?"

If you see enough photos and videos of the supposed moon landing you can find many, many, anomalies that just should not be there.

For example, there is a clear letter "C" on one of the moon rocks and another smaller "c" right in front of the rock. Many have speculated that this is a stage prop that tells a stage hand where to place the rock on the sound stage or studio where they were filming.

Others have seen spotlights reflecting off the visors of astronauts in some pictures. This spotlights are actually the big bright studio lights that are used when all the footage was filmed and the photos shot.

In addition, some have even noticed shadows on the ceiling detected in computer enhancement when the Lunar Extraction Module is being lifted up or supposedly taking off from the moon.

There are videos on YouTube, where a person on his

computer, shows a picture of the Earth and the Moon taken by the Apollo astronauts and by using Adobe Photo shop, and adjusting saturation levels, he demonstrates, a rectangular area where the picture of Earth was clearly cropped into the picture.

To add to the hoax, there are other countries faking their own lunar excursions, including the Chinese, albeit not as convincing as the Americans. It is only a matter of time, when one of the space Agencies from China, Russia or the United States will flagrantly mess up and blow this entire hoax of space travel wide open.

The Chinese also sent a rover to the moon, and very recently, I might add. They ended up uploading the video of their lunar rover online, but only for a short time, and then they decided to pull it down. The reason, is because the experts all were finding many discrepancies, once again with the Chinese rover and the lunar surface itself. Moreover, they did not find the American flag or rover on the moon which should still be there, according to NASA.

No stars were found either in their pictures.How convenient! NASA must have trained them well.

Continuing with stockpiling evidence and uncanny events or phenomenon against NASA, I would like to present one fantastic and surreal admission from NASA. So apparently, NASA claims that they accidentally deleted all the Moon landing videos by mistake. In an article entitled "Houston, we have a problem: original moon walk footage erased." NASA stated that "in the scientific equivalent of recording an old episode of EastEnders over the prized video of your daughter's wedding day, NASA probably taped over its only high-resolution images of the first moon walk with electronic data from a satellite or a later manned space mission, officials said today."

"But a standard NASA money-saving measure in those days was to reuse the 14-inch tape reels after several years in storage. Agency officials ultimately concluded that the original 11 tapes were buried among an estimated 350,000 that were recycled in the 1970s and 1980s and the data was lost forever," the article stated.

There is another video that helps debunk astronauts going to the moon.

The video that I am referring to shows the Extra Vehicular Mobility Unit/ EMU, or space suit, and the man in the video does a great job in explaining just how difficult it is for one person to don the suit by himself. He goes on to explain that one astronaut by himself, really needs at least two people or assistants to help him don the space suit.

There are many pieces to this suit but the reason I bring it up here is because you have to remember how tiny the LEM really is. "Of all the pictures of the lunar module commonly accompanying articles about the Apollo lunar landings, none really show just how tiny the spacecraft was. It was tiny, with its legs extended it stood 22 feet and 11 inches tall with a diameter of 31 feet measured diagonally between footpads." And it was made of two parts. The lower descent stage whose main engine slowed the spacecraft to a soft landing then acted as a launch platform for the ascent stage to propel the crew back into lunar orbit at the end of their stay on the surface." I found this article in Popular Science magazine article entitled, "Seeing Inside the Apollo Lunar Module."

In this article it stipulates the crew compartment was just "12 feet and 4 inches tall and 14 feet and 1 inch in diameter. There weren't any seats for the crew."

What I want to know, is how in the heck did both Neil Armstrong and Buzz Aldrin don their 185pound spacesuits, without any assistants, and in such confined spaces?

How is this even possible? I mean they have the undergarment, the adult size diaper, and the cooling suit, along with the cooling tubes to connect to the outer suit. Then they have to jump into the big Space suit in two pieces. First the bottom torso and then the upper part. Then they have to secure the gloves which twist on and off, but before that, they have to secure the face piece which consists of several layers to block out the sun, and then don the helmet. Oh and I forgot the space boots that they wore. On top of all this they have to take out the Hasselblad camera and mount it to the space suit of Neil Armstrong, because there is no way that he had the camera already mounted to the space suit inside the module.

I find this task nearing the improbable, except if they were donning the spacesuit inside of a studio to take pictures as part of a hoax, then yes I believe it.

Ralph Rene, did an experiment where he added the same amount of clothes to simulate a space suit weight of 185 pounds, and then he tried to crawl under his dining room table which was about the same size as the LEM compartment and he could not fit under it and accomplish this task.

David Percy also measured the clearance of the width of the hatch (Dark Moon, p.341) and he says that "egress would be very difficult."

James Collier asserts that "NASA did not provide the astronauts with any instruction manual for getting out of the LEM around that inward-opening door."

However, NASA expects us to believe that the astronauts could have figured out the hatch once they arrived on the moon.

Still as a final note, one of the most definitive proofs of trickery from NASA is the lack of stars in any of the Moon photos.

The reason is because it would be easy for an astronomer or a well-trained person to measure the angularity of the stars behind the earth, for example, in a photo, so they decided not to add stars to any of the pictures from the Moon landings.

I know that many people will often play the "credibility card" on Moon Hoax investigators.

In other words, they will suggest that the people that are

exposing the truth are a bunch of conspiracy theorists and crackpots.

What about our former President Bill Clinton? He is someone with credibility right? I mean he was our President for two terms!

"Just a month before, Apollo 11 astronauts Buzz Aldrin and Neil Armstrong had left their colleague, Michael Collins, aboard spaceship Columbia and walked on the Moon. The old carpenter asked me if I really believed it happened. I said sure, I saw it on television. He disagreed; he said that he didn't believe it for a minute, that 'them television fellers' could make things look real that weren't. Back then, I thought he was a crank. During my eight years in Washington, I saw some things on TV that made me wonder if he wasn't ahead of his time."

— President Bill Clinton

Is it all that hard to believe that our government would lie or fake something to accomplish what they think is for the greater good?

How many of you have heard about the Ghost Army deception unit during World War II?

Wikipedia says that there were about 1100 men in this unit and their sole mission was to impersonate other U.S. Army units.

Megan Garber describes in "Ghost Army: The Inflatable Tanks That Fooled Hitler," the following:

"From a few week after D-Day, when they landed in France, until the end of the war, they put on a 'traveling road show' utilizing inflatable tanks, sound trucks, fake radio transmissions and pretense. They staged more than 20 battlefield deceptions, often operating very close to the front lines. Their story was kept secret for more than 40 years after the war, and elements of it remain classified."

So we can see that deception has been part of our government's "bag of tricks" for a long time.

Is it really that difficult to believe that a great illusion can mystify and intrigue the "Captivated Audience?

And like a great magician, the trickery and illusions seem to work wonders.

On closing for this chapter, I'd like to include how some people will say that NASA astronauts brought back hundreds of pounds of Moon rock to study. However, according to a London telegraph article entitled "'Moon rock' given to Holland by Neil Armstrong and Buzz Aldrin is fake," the piece of Moon rock ended up being a piece of petrified wood.

7

HELIOCENTRIC OR GEOCENTRIC MODEL OF EARTH

Heliocentric or Geocentric Model of Earth

I would like to begin this chapter, by asking you a series of questions first.

"Do you believe that we live on a spinning Earth?"

"Can you prove that gravity exists?"

"How do you know?"

"How do the people in Australia stand up without falling off the Earth?" I mean think about it, if we live in the U.S.A. on the North American continent, then Australia is upside down on a ball earth right?

"How does the water in the oceans stay in the oceans without falling off into space?"

If your answer to my first question is a resounding "Yes" and that you believe the globe Earth model, then you, my dear friend, fall with the rest of the 85 % of the population. Firstly, I want to explain a little bit about this model of Earth.

This model of the Solar system is called the heliocentric model. In this model of the earth, "You" believe that the sun is the center of the solar system.

I don't blame you for believing this model, since at an early stage in our life, "We" are all taught to believe that the sun is the center of our solar system.

We are told that a collection of planets orbit this star, (the sun), including Earth. Furthermore, our solar system is in the Milky Way galaxy, "which is within a universe of galaxies called the local cluster which is lost in the vastness of space, like a grain of sand in the Sahara desert," according to Phillip Stott, a professor at the University of London.

The acceptance of the Earth being a round shape and that it spins on its axis is the normal and accepted belief of the entire world.

I have heard it explained as the rotundity of the earth, which just means that it is round, supposedly. Any model is based on a certain set of observations. A "good model" must be able to explain as many characteristics of these observations as possible, but also be as simple as possible. This definition is found on the Annenberg Learner website.

The issue that I have about this Earth model, is the supposed fact includes all of these statements:

• The "Big Bang Universe" happened out of one singularity event that expanded over 13.82 billion years to where we are today.

• We came from nothing except energy and matter and by some inexplicable random event, dark energy, along with gravity and relativity formed our universe and planets and stars. Then atoms just started forming together and formed a single cell organism which eventually formed a two cell organism and then through evolution, humans evolved from apes.

• We are insignificant beings when compared to the billions of stars and galaxies and planets in the ever expanding universe.

Even the Disney Channel wants you to believe that we are an insignificant species. Let me explain.

One day, I was watching a show on Disney called "Best Friends Whenever", with my 10 year old step son, and on the show, two kids were sitting at a table on one of the episodes.

Reynaldo, who is one of the boys, in the conversation, says to Barry, another boy in the cafeteria, that he has been thinking about Barry's problem, to which Barry interjects with "what, the fact that I'm alone and an insignificant being in the vast an infinite expanse of the cosmos?" end quote...Reynaldo, quickly answers "that will never change." End quote.

The sound of laughter in the background, dismisses the austerity of this moronic statement.

I wanted to throw this in here, just so you can see that the broadcasting of some popular secular shows on television is used effectively to help brain wash young people around the earth. This truly is indoctrination 101 and it is relentless; After all, young minds are easy to mold.

In order to be able to compare how this transformation and indifferent world came into being, we must first visit and learn from history.

I would now, like to first compare the way people all the way up until the 17th century trusted their own observations when it came to space, and religion.

But then some "pseudo science" changed all this.

For about 6000 years or more, many religions around the world believed that the earth was flat.

What is so astounding to me, is how eerily similar the big picture of the earth really was in the beliefs across the many different religions across the world. They may have worshipped different gods, but the general consensus was that the earth was the center of the universe and that it was flat. This can even be seen in hieroglyphics in caves and paintings of ancient cultures.

The Chinese, for example, believed and described the heavens as being like an umbrella covering the earth (the

Kai Tian theory).

In a passage of Zhang Heng's cosmogony Zhang himself says :

"Heaven takes its body from the Yang, so it is round and in motion. Earth takes its body from the Yin, so it is flat and quiescent," from an article "Flat Earth" in Wikipedia.

The cultures around the world that believed the flat earth model included the following countries: Greece, India, Egypt, and China. The ancient Norse and Germanic and aboriginal cultures also believed.

In early Mesopotamian mythology, the world was portrayed as a flat disk floating in the ocean and surrounded by a spherical sky, according to Wikipedia.

As an interjection here, I started to compare the similarities with the ancient view of the earth and I noticed that the earth looked more and more like the "Biblical Earth"!

(I will devote an entire chapter to the Biblical earth.)

What happened to this wonderful view of the earth as the geocentric model where the earth is the center of the galaxy?

Science is what happened! Not all science is bad, only the unproven theoretical science, the kind that alienated us away from God. It is a demonic agenda that accomplished this doctrine under the guise of Academia.

I remember when I was in school, and we covered the topic of the earth being flat, I remember how ignorant I thought these people were. (As the saying goes, "hindsight is 20/

20," and I thank God that I see the truth now.)

Of course, in school, we were taught that if a ship went too far, on the flat earth, it would fall off over the edge into space. I was too young, and my mind could easily be molded to conform to the status quo.

Teachers, after all, don't know any better than to teach what they have been indoctrinated to teach by the accepted truths of science from the Freemason's Academia.

Part of my book's message and theme is about challenging the Status Quo!

This is where, my book really gets interesting and challenging. I hope you really pay attention to every word that follows here. It involves how science is used to control our minds.

Evolution, for example, was one of the main scientific unproven conundrums that began the entire paradigm shift of a flat earth to the heliocentric model. Maybe it should be called the "Hell-o-centric Model."

The 18th century is what began, what I call the "Evolution Revolution."

This is the time when some brilliant minds, whom all happen to be Freemasons, by the way, invented concepts like evolution, gravity, and relativity to name a few of the world altering notions and laws.

Isn't it a coincidence that all three of the laws of science came from Freemasons?

Thomas Huxley was a member of the British Royal

Society, which was made up of only freemasons. He is an influential friend that encouraged Charles Darwin to come out with his theory of Evolution, of which was somewhat started by Darwin's grandfather Erasmus.

Things really fell into place for the elite when they created the Royal Society of London.

I found it amusing and ironic that their motto is the following:

Their motto "Nullius in verba" means "take nobody's word for it."

Unfortunately, for the social masses, "We" all have to take "Their" word for it and believe all the Pseudo-science bull like the fact that they can pin point to a trillionth of a second the formation of the universe from the singularity event, that supposedly was the Big Bang Theory!

Please give me a break!

This establishment of the British Royal Society empowered the elite and logistically placed them to be sort of the gate keepers for the establishment of whatever Academia and prestigious clubs they wanted to accept and peddle to the masses.

For the following discussion, I am borrowing information from an article written by Phillip D. Collins entitled "The Ascendancy of the Scientific Dictatorship

Part One: Illuminating the Occult Origin of Darwinism."

The article, basically explains the formation of what is essentially a Cartel that acts as powerful entity (the elite), however, one big difference is that they control science and information instead of drugs.

Also, I will introduce the term "Scientific Dictatorship" in this article.

"In The Architecture of Modern Political Power, Daniel Pouzzner outlines the tactics employed by the elite to maintain their dominance. Among them is: 'Ostensible control over the knowable, by marketing institutionally accredited science as the only path to true understanding' (Pouzzner, 75). Thus the ruling class endeavors to discourage independent reason while exercising illusory power over human knowledge. This tactic of control through knowledge suppression and selective dissemination is reiterated in the anonymously authored document Silent Weapons for Quiet Wars.:

Energy is recognized as the key to all activity on earth. Natural science is the study of the sources and control of natural energy, and social science, theoretically expressed as economics, is the study of the sources and control of social energy. Both are bookkeeping systems. Mathematics is the primary energy science. And the bookkeeper can be king if the public can be kept ignorant of the methodology of the bookkeeping. All science is merely a means to an end. The means is knowledge. The end is control.

After all, remember the purpose of the Royal Society, according to Webster Tarpley in How the Venetian System Was Transplanted into England, he states that "Metaphysical naturalism (i.e. nature is God) had to be enthroned. .

68

Meanwhile, God's presence in the corridors of science had to be expunged. To achieve this, the Royal Society created a Gnostic division between science and theology thus insuring the primacy of matter in the halls of scientific inquiry (Tarpley 1996)."

The article "Scientific Dictatorship" continues with what I believe is the cut and dry purpose of the creation of the ape-man in evolution. The Ascendancy of the Scientific Dictatorship Part One: Illuminating the Occult Origin of Darwinism. Collins once again highlights the main agenda of the Illuminati and I quote the following:

Recall the words of Aldous Huxley in Brave New World Revisited: 'the older dictators fell because they could never supply enough bread, enough circuses, enough miracles and mysteries.' The new dictators do not intend to make the same mistake. With the effective enshrinement of metaphysical naturalism, the British Society prepared to unleash their next golem. [in occult text, the golem was an artificially created man whose life was the result of supernatural intervention] However, this golem would be an artificially created ape-man presented to the public imagination under the appellation of Darwinism.

In this very insightful article that I have been quoting, the following section really explains the ultimate goal of the Freemasons.

How did the "scientific dictatorship" of the twentieth century begin? In earlier centuries, the ruling class controlled the masses through more mystical belief systems particularly Sun worship.

Remember, the earlier story of how Pharaoh took credit for the sun rising every day and also for eclipses of the Moon?

Yet this would all change. In Saucers of the Illuminati, Jim Keith documents the shift from a theocracy of the Sun to a theocracy of "science":

Since the Sun God (and his various relations, including sons and wives) were, after several thousand years of worship, beginning to fray around the edges in terms of believability, and a lot of commoners were beginning to grumble that this stuff was all made up, the Illuminati came up with a new and improved version of their mind control software that didn't depend upon the Sun God or Moon Goddess for ultimate authority.

– Keith, Saucers of the Illuminati, 78

Priests and rituals were soon supplanted by a new breed of bookkeepers and a new "methodology of bookkeeping"

Keith elaborates:

As the Sun/Moon cult lost some of its popularity, "Scientists" were quick to take up some of the slack. According to their propaganda, the physical laws of the universe were the ultimate causative factors, and naturally, those physical laws were only fathomable by the scientific (i.e. Illuminati) elite.

— Keith, Saucers of the Illuminati, 78-79

However, if we look at a passage of the Bible in, 1 Timothy

4:2 in the Bible says the following:

"Such teachings come through hypocritical liars, whose consciences have been seared as with a hot iron."

500 years later we the Flat Earth proponents and I, are still having to expose and explain to the masses the huge deception that enslaves them.

Having shown you what I believe to be the climax, of my book, I want to shift gears and return to the subject of this chapter.

I want to share an article by Lee Holmes entitled "Copernicus, Galileo, and Darwin—Three Men Who Changed the World," and it explained the who's who of the heliocentric earth model, and their contributions.

One of the main advocate of the spinning earth model and who is mentioned in the annals of astronomy was Nicolaus Copernicus, a Polish astronomer who produced a workable model of the solar system. (1473-1543).

However, according to Diogenes Laertius, "Pythagoras was the first Greek who called the Earth round."

The telescope had not even been invented yet, and so all of Copernicus' observations, were performed and documented by just the naked eye.

The same article by Holmes, goes on to say also that "around 1517 Copernicus began writing his major work and his theory was that the Earth rotates daily on its axis and revolves around the sun yearly. This is the heliocentric system, and it challenged the Ptolemaic theory that the Earth was the center of the Universe, the geocentric model."

Johannes Kepler was another major player in changing the geocentric view by turning the paradigm from the earth as the center of the universe– to the sun being the center of the universe.

In an article I read entitled The Biblical Flat Earth: The Illuminati Agenda, Phillip Stallings writes that "The heliocentric position is certainly connected to sun worship which goes all the way back to Nimrod and [the] tower of Babel. This system of worship has its origin in the legend of Nimrod and his wife Semiramus. Nimrod (the great-grandson of Noah) rebelled against God, like his father Cush. Eventually Nimrod was put to death for his evil

deeds, and according to the ancient patriarchal system, parts of his body were sent to various cities as a warning."

Nimrod has been said to be the founder of Masonry. I will reference this passage again in my chapter about the Illuminati and Symbolism. Here, we can start to understand, the use of the symbolism of the sun, which the Illuminati honor and revere. Is it a far stretch to see why they chose the Sun to be the center of our galaxy?

Quoting from Lee Holmes', article "Kepler discovered that planets move in elliptical orbits. "In his 'Epitome of Copernican Astronomy', Kepler fully laid out a new heliocentric model for the universe with the planets on elliptical orbits."

Galileo was the first person to use the telescope in the

study of astronomy. "Until 1632, the heliocentric theory was easily dismissed because there was no explanation for why the Earth does not appear to move. Galileo explained this using his principle of relativity, which stated that all uniform motion is relative and there is no absolute state of rest." I found this information from Heliocentric models of the Solar System. Section 2.4 Galileo and the telescope. Nick Kanas (author) tells us that "Ancient Greek mathematician Pythagoras was the first to suggest that the Earth is spherical in about 500 BC, and this was accepted by most Greek philosophers at the time."

In 1916 Isaac Newton gave birth to the mysterious force called "gravity." His law of gravitation was instrumental in the scientific revolution. This theory is one of the biggest unexplained phenomenon to date.

I mean, are you going to believe that gravity is what holds the water in the oceans and also that gravity is what causes the curvature of the earth? Do you remember my preface about one theory that begat another theory?

The amount of force that this gravitational force would require to keep water in the ocean and cause the curvature of the Earth, should pin down any object or human being on it, and render them immoveable. In other words, a person should not be able to walk, run, swim and throw a football, or be able to splash water in a pool by simply running their hands across the water. But we are able to do all of these things, and without very much effort. I am simply introducing ideas to make you think about here.

Another interesting observation that I found today, comes from a video entitled Flat Earth explained by David Murphy Pt 1 on YouTube. Murphy very eloquently explains that if the earth is an Oblate spheroid like Neil Degrasse Tyson proposes, then due to centripetal force of the earth spinning faster at the equator than at the poles, the water in the oceans on earth should have accumulated at the equator and there should not be land located there. An example he suggested to help us envision this is, if you wet a tennis ball and then spin it fast, and slow down the video in slow motion you can see where all the water molecules collect and emit from the center of the ball. The same phenomena should occur on a ball Earth. Obviously this does not happen. However, I would like to return the focus back to the heliocentric and geocentric model of earth.

Newton, a natural philosopher supported Kepler's findings. But Newton proposed that matter essentially pulled on other matter in space. In addition, according to an article entitled "Strange but True: Earth is Not Round," Charles Q. Choi, states that Newton, was one of the first to predict the oblate spheroid shape of the earth. (Maybe, this is why current scientists and the Freemasonic NASA push the shape of earth as an oblate spheroid).

However, I want to add his definition of what an oblate spheroid looks like. Choi states that "Isaac Newton first proposed that Earth was not perfectly round. Instead, he suggested it was an oblate spheroid-a sphere that is squashed at

its poles and swollen at the equator. He was correct and, because of this bulge, the distance from Earth's center to sea level is roughly 21 kilometers (13 miles) greater at the equator than at the poles."

But as a very important note here to add, later on in his life, Newton became president of the Royal Society.

Notice a pattern here? Strange coincidence, or structured society rewarding their fellow members?

Yet another theory that begat another theory is concerned, let us now introduce relativity really quickly here.

In 1916 Albert Einstein's theory of General Relativity made the heliocentric model fit by expounding on the theory of gravity. Einstein theories explained some of Newton's findings. One major difference according to

Einstein's Theory of Relativity about matter, was that Einstein proposed that matter actually distorts space-time and it is this distortion that affects other matter.

In other words, the Theory of Relativity postulated that the gravitational force of big masses or planets is actually due to the curvature of the empty space.

In this website article entitled astronomy.nmsu.edu it states that "There are other forces in nature, gravity is the weakest of all of nature's forces, but because the others are strong, and have both positive and negative charges, they quickly cancel themselves out. Gravity is an odd force in that it is only attractive—thus even though it is weak, it is the force that controls how matter behaves in our Universe."

In article on website space.com entitled "Einstein's Theory of General Relativity," it states that "Although instruments can neither see nor measure space-time, several of the phenomena predicted by its warping have been confirmed."

This is the kind of pseudo-science that they try to use to brain wash the masses into believing all the theories that have been created to explain how the universe works and continue to push the heliocentric model.

I think the theory of relativity fits in perfectly with science fiction and one great movie "Interstellar" really expounds on the fabric of time and the speed of light, quantum mechanics, quarks, and the jargon about multiple universes.

However, it would be interesting to know where we would be today, if the hot air balloon was invented or the airplane, rockets or any object that could go up high and capture the non-existent curvature of the Earth, the true Biblical Earth model would reign supreme.

However, when you do see this curvature it is because of what they call "fish eyed" lenses being used to shoot the video which are on many of the famous GoPro cameras. In other words, the camera that is being used probably has a fish eyed lens and so when they try to shoot a panoramic view of the horizon, a curvature is noticeable due to the lens and not due to the curve of the earth. One easy way to disprove this, is when the video of the supposed curvature is seen, check to see if you can see the curvature towards the horizon whenever, the object that is headed to space is only a few hundred feet up. If the horizon looks curved already and not in space yet, then that is usually what it is. Someone actually said that you can see the curvature of the earth from a plane, but I have been on planes plenty and all I see is a flat horizon. Eric Dubay says that regardless of where you are on Earth, the horizon always rises relative to your position. The higher you go, the horizon also rises with you, which would not be the case if the Earth was curved.

I have a great example to add to this chapter and I hope you really allow it to soak into your brain. I found a video where Neil Degrasse Tyson came out on a show on YouTube called the Anthony Cumia Show, and they were talking about the Flat Earth as being a joke. He goes on to use the tallest building in the world, the Burj Khalifa in Dubai, as an example of the curvature of the

Earth. Neil Degrasse Tyson says that the people that are on the very top of the building can actually see the sunset for 2 extra minutes longer than the people at the bottom. His answer, is that it is due to the curvature of the Earth.

Now it is my turn to explain what is happening here. On our Flat Earth, a person at ground level can see about 3 miles to the horizon. When a person goes up in elevation or altitude, i.e. on an airplane or hot air balloon, the horizon rises to a person's eye level and you are able to view far greater distances to the horizon.

I have already ran some numbers, and this is what you will notice. If you are at 35,000 feet up in the air, for example, the cruising altitude on a commercial airliner, then you should be able to see 229.3 miles to the horizon. If you climb mount Everest which is about 5 miles high or about 30 to 31,000 feet, a person could see approximately 208 miles to the horizon.

The building we are using here, has 2 levels for observing the panaromic breath-taking view in Dubai. One is Level 125 and is the one that I will use to make my point across. This level sits 1496 feet, or 456 meters. A person at this height can see 47.4 miles to the horizon versus the measly 3 miles for the folks at the bottom levels.

In this scenario, let us calculate the speed of the Sun first. On a Flat Earth it travels at 1035 miles per hour or 17.25 miles per minute. So what is happening here is that when the people at the top (at Level 125) can see the sun for an extra 2 minutes, it is because the sun has traveled 34.5 miles away in 2 minutes. (17.25 miles per minute x 2 minutes = 34.5 miles) and since these people at the top can see up to 47 miles, due to the height that they are at, these people are able to see the sun for the 2 extra minutes; 2.8 minutes to be exact, whereas the people at the bottom can only see 3 miles off to the horizon due to the vantage point, the sun seems to disappear quicker for them into the horizon i.e. sunset.

This explains exactly what is observed versus the "Ball Earth," curvature explanation, wouldn't you agree?

8

FREEMASONS AND THE ILLUMINATI

———————

Freemasons and the Illuminati

In this chapter the occult nature of Freemasons and the Illuminati will be exposed.

In his conclusion about the illuminati, in The Aim of Freemasonry is the Triumph of Communism, Dr. Henry Makow states the following: "We have been born into the seventh or eighth inning of a nine inning Game and God is trailing badly. The Illuminati have defined God in nonsensical terms and thus banished Him from our universe. God is synonymous with spiritual ideals. Instead of man making his rendezvous with the Creator, we are being degraded and turned into animals, better to serve the illuminati."

Eric Dubay expounds on this same lines on The FlatEarth Conspiracy by saying that "they trap us in the ballEarth delusion as children before we're old enough to question it, then by the time we are, we're too

indoctrinated to care and just go about ridiculing anyone who presents us with the truth."

Just how secretive and clandestine is this organization? I am not inferring that the assassination of President John f. Kennedy was a conspiracy orchestrated by the elites, I am merely presenting a quote that I want to share. I found a quote by President Kennedy and it was foreboding and coincidental in his demise. "There's a plot in this country to enslave every man, woman and child. Before I leave this high and noble office, I intend to expose this plot."

This was 7 days before his assassination.

In Dr. Makow's article published December 2015, he states that there are 5 million Freemason members and 3 million in the U.S. He says that in The Protocols of the Elders of Zion, it states in Protocol 15 that "we shall create and multiply free Masonic lodges... absorb into them all who may become or who are prominent in public activity, for in these lodges we shall find our principle intelligence office and means of influence... The most secret political plots, will be known to us and will fall under our guiding hands... We know the final goal...whereas the goyim have knowledge of nothing..."

94

In addition, it goes on to say that, "Gentile masonry blindly serves as a screen for us and our objects, but the plan of action of our force, even its very abiding place, remains for the whole people and unknown mystery. Who and what is in a position to overthrow an invisible force?" (Protocol 4).

The Illuminati's conspiracy is to ring in a New World Order.

What is the New World Order?

I believe that by quoting directly from the description of Dr. Makow's book Illuminati3: Satanic Possession: There is only one Conspiracy that it will give us an overall short synapsis of the world agenda and the separation of the people that are in the "Know" and all the rest of us. The author states the following: "Western society is based on a rebellion against God and the natural and moral order. The so called 'Enlightenment' refers to Lucifer as the 'light giver.' Satanist (Cabalist) Jews and Freemasons are waging a covert war against God and man and are close to achieving victory. Many Jews and Freemasons have been a subversive force throughout history- the real reason for anti-Semitism. Of course, the majority of Jews (and Christians) aren't aware of this process of satanic possession. We have all succumbed to it. Passing as 'secularism' and 'humanism,' Satanism is the secret religion of the West."

In a website called www.gotquestions.org, in a blog entitled "What is the New World Order?" the writer says that "The appeal of this New World Order lies in its proposal to free the world of wars and political strife, and it promises to eradicated poverty, disease, and hunger. Its purpose if to meet the needs and hopes of all mankind through worldwide peace."

The article continues by warning us that "History has proven time and again that no quasi-world empire has ever survived, simply because of it innate flaws of greed, corruption, and quest for power."

Moreover, the author writes that "false religious teachings cannot bring utopia into being, regardless of man's creativity and ingenuity. Only heaven brings lasting peace and happiness."

In the final conclusion, I agree 110 % with what the author says when he says "Yes, hope is needed. But it is the hope of heaven we need, not the false hope of a New World Oder. The one hope for all believers lies only in heaven (John 14:1-4). It is not here on this earth."

The main agenda of the Illuminati according to Phillip 96 Stalling in The Biblical Flat Earth: The Illuminati Agenda is "solely to try and disprove the Bible the same as with the lie of evolution. We know Satan is the 'father of lies' and seeks to deceive through counterfeit schemes and agendas (John 8:44)" and continuing from this article:

"Furthermore, the position of flying through space while

orbiting the sun, headed to nowhere exactly, is what really devalues and distracts from God's creation and human life. The earth is reduced to happenstance and insignificance in light of the unending universe of space, planets and the stars. Humanity appears to be a cosmic accident rather than a beautifully designed creation of God."

I read the discussion that Philip Stallings proposes and I must say, it is an eye opener and very well written.

He basically introduces the formation of an Illuminati group starting with "The Jason Society" which was formed by President Eisenhower in 1957. During this time frame there were various very important happenings that set into motion the current agenda of the Freemasons.

Let us begin with the first major event.

"Operation Fishbowl" was an operation where the United States launched nuclear test bombs up in the sky between 1958 and 1962 in the vicinity of Johnston Island,

The Captivated Audience: Hoaxes, Illusions and the Biblical Earth

near Hawaii. I believe that this is when the elite realized that we are under a firmament as is written in the bible, hence the name "Fishbowl."

Still, another major event that occurred, and which made me believe in the Flat Earth, is the signing of the Antarctic Treaty. In Phillip Stallings' The Biblical Flat Earth: The Illuminati Agenda, it was "signed in Washington on December 1st, 1959 by the twelve countries whose scientists had been active in and around Antarctica during the International Geophysical Year (IGY) of 1957-58. It entered into force in 1961 and has since been acceded to by many other nations. The total number of Parties to the Treaty are now 53. Antarctica represents the very edge of the flat earth."

I will cover Antarctica in chapter 8 of the book.

"The elites believe the earth, that is enclosed, has too many people. They believe they must maintain balance between the numbers of people vs the amount of resources available." Quote from the same article.

Furthermore, the author of this article adds that all the various population control tactics are employed and include the following: chemtrails, abortion (infanticide), wars in the Middle East, multiculturalism, and vaccines. 98

I would like to cover the occult symbols that the Illuminati use since we are on this chapter and topic.

In this chapter I want to use a quote that David J. Stewart uses in his website about symbolism:

"Symbolism is the language of the Mysteries. By symbols men have ever sought to communicate to each other those thoughts which transcend the limitations of language. Rejecting man-conceived dialects as inadequate and unworthy to perpetuate divine ideas, the Mysteries thus chose symbolism as a far more ingenious and ideal method of preserving their transcendental knowledge. In a single figure a figure may both reveal and conceal, for to the wise the subject of the symbol is obvious, while to the ignorant the figure remains inscrutable. Hence, he who seeks to unveil the secret doctrine of antiquity mush search for that doctrine not upon the open pages of books which might fall into the hands of the unworthy but in the place where it was originally concealed."

– Manly P. Hall, The Secret Teachings of all Ages, p. 20.

I will be quoting extensively from this great article entitled Symbols of the Illuminati, by David J. Stewart.

He explains the following:

"From messages delivered to the masses through the media and films to Time Warner's all-seeing eye, we are repeatedly reminded by the Illuminati themselves that they are controlling us and are omnipresent. World leaders from Bill Clinton, to Prince William have been photographed proudly flashing the sign of the Devil." It is the sign that looks like flashing the Texas Longhorns symbol with your hand but it is paying homage to the prince of darkness. You can add all of the following to the list that have flashed the symbol repeatedly: Michelle and Barack Obama, Bill and Hillary Clinton, Beyonce, Michael Jackson, Barbara Bush, Gene Simmons, Dave Navarro, Quentin Tarantino, and the list goes on and on.

Stewart explains that the all-seeing eye essentially can be referenced to the beginning of time in Genesis. When "the Serpent promised Adam and Eve that their eyes would 'be opened' if they ate of the fruit of the tree of knowledge of good and evil. The key word in this passage is eyes, which in Hebrew can be translated 'knowledge.' Opened can be translated 'broadened.' What the Serpent promised Adam and Eve was that knowledge would be broadened if they ate of the forbidden fruit.

But the most foreboding aspect of this Scripture emerges from the fact that the Hebrew word for 'eyes' is not plural but singular. What the Serpent actually told Adam and Eve was that their 'eye' would be broadened by knowledge. The 'eye' that Scripture wants us to consider is not the physical organ of sight, but the eye of the mind or the soul. This singular 'eye' is called the 'third eye' of clairvoyance in the Hindu religion, the eye of Osiris in Egypt, and the All-Seeing Eye in Freemasonry. (Source: John Daniel, Scarlet and the Beast, Volume III, pp. 6-7)."

The symbols that I want to discuss in my book are found in the One dollar bill.

The One Dollar bill seal with the "All-Seeing Eye" above the Pyramid. "The eye represents the illuminati ruling from their position on the capstone of the pyramid. They are very few at the top while we are many at the bottom. The all-seeing eye on the pyramid was added to the reverse side of the Great Seal of the United States and finally adopted by Congress in 1782. In 1935, President and 33rd degree Freemason, Franklin Roosevelt added the front and back of

the Seal to the one dollar bill." I obtained this information from A Complete Guide to Illuminati

Symbols, Signs, and Meanings.

Also the Latin Novus Ordo Seclorum means Secular New Order. Secular means not pertaining to religion. The Annuit Coeptis writing on the One Dollar Bill translates to "announcing conception."

Combine the two words and this means "Announcing the conception of a Secular New Order."

In Occult Numerology of World Events a blog by Mr. Rockwell, he explains the enigmatic code of the number system that the Illuminati uses. For example, Rockwell states that "3 is the first sacred number. It is a perfect number representing the pagan trinity. It geometrically represents the triangle, the pyramid and spiritually, the third eye. Sacred numbers are intensified when grouped. 33 is a very powerful number to occultists. There are 33 degrees in Freemasonry which symbolizes the Kundalini or 'serpent force' which is directed up the 33 sections of the vertebrae to achieve 'illumination.' 666 is achieved when 3 groups of 3 are added together (3+3) + (3+3) +(3+3)= 666."

102

"13" sounds like just a number, however, it is used to represent the 13 Illuminati bloodlines/families which collectively rule the planet.

There are 13 layers of Brick on the Pyramid itself.

The Eagle seal on the opposite side of the Pyramid, has 13 illuminated stars and 13 letters in the motto "E Pluribus Unum" which means one of many. There are 13 arrows,

---

and 13 leaves that the eagle is holding.

In the article, A Complete guide to Illuminati Symbols, Signs and Meanings, it explains that "Skulls are used as a reminder of death in Freemasonry and for the Skull and Bones. Young initiates are reminded that they only have a short life to work towards the eternal illuminati's goal."

The MDCCLXXVI is Roman Number "1776", which is the date the Illuminati formed. The year 1776 represent the founding of the Bavarian Illuminati by Adam Weishaupt.

The Statue of Liberty holding the torch with flame, was designed by Freemason, Frederic Bartholdi. The name of Lucifer literally means "bringer of light." So you see the connection here.

Revelation 13:18 (NKJV) "Let him who has understanding calculate the number of the beast, for it is the number of a man. His number is 666."

Finally, in the Top Ten Illuminati Symbols that I found on www.illuminatirex.com, article it says that "the number of the Beast is associated with the Anti-Christ who would eventually take helm of the illuminati as he brings forth the New World Order. The music industry is a prime recruiting ground for the Illuminati. Illuminated musicians incorporate Illuminati symbolism in their work as a nudge to their Illuminati handlers."

A quick example is a rap song by Jay-Z "Empire State of mind" he says, "And Jesus can't save you, life starts when the church ends." What do you think he means by saying this?

A very puzzling thing happened to me today as I wrote these lines, on May 10th 2016.

I know it is relative to the book and so I am sharing it with you.

I was getting pictures for my book cover today and I wanted it to contain something with earth and the moon or astronauts. I was using my Samsung phone to surf the web. As I was parked in my truck during my lunch break at work, I found a great picture that I am sure you have seen before, and it has a big moon, but only the top quarter of it. It also

104

has the LEM coming down or orbiting the moon and in the background you can see the small earth in the distance. As I hit download to save this image to my phone this is what the name of the file was:

69666main_Apollo-fig7.gif file. I am not making this up! It gave me goosebumps!

I had to re-download the file because I could not read the name of the file when I was looking for it. However,

The Captivated Audience: Hoaxes, Illusions and the Biblical Earth

hopefully you can go to www.pics-about-space.com and be able to find this gif file under this name.

"Jesus said in John 18:20, 'I spake openly to the world..in secret have I said nothing.' This is in sharp contrast to secret societies which operate in secrecy. The reason why occult groups, such as Freemasonry, must operate in secrecy is because their works are evil. If the public knew what the predatory ruling elite were planning for the world, there'd be massive hangings by sunset. To educate yourself on the subject, watch the free eye-opening and shocking Alex Jones' documentary movie.. END GAMEBlueprint for Global Enslavement." Still quoting from

David J. Stewart article.

Walt Disney was a 33rd degree Freemason and Disneyland has a "Club 33." The Magic Kingdom castle was designed after Bavaria's Neuschwanstein Castle where the Illuminati was formed.

In 13 Illuminati Bloodlines, Fritz Springmeier, made me cringe, when I read all that he stipulates about the families and descendants of the Illuminati. He says that the families were chosen by Satan himself. In case you are wondering, according to Fritz the families involved are the following: the Astor bloodline, the Bundy bloodline, the Collins

bloodline, the Dupont bloodline, the Freeman bloodline, the Kennedy bloodline, the Li bloodline, the Onassis bloodline, the Rockefeller bloodline, the Rothschild bloodline, the Russell bloodline, the Van Duyn bloodline and the Merovingian bloodline.

According to an article I found called The Richest Family in the World, by Matt Blitz, The Rothschild family, descendants of Mayer A. Rothschild, is still around today and is believed to be worth over a trillion dollars combined, thought to be the largest private fortunate in the history of the world."

In an earlier chapter, if you remember, I'd mentioned Nimrod being the founder of Freemasonry, I said I would relate it to this chapter about symbolism and the Illuminati. Well here it is. According to Fritz's article, he informs us that the Rothschilds are able to trace their heritage to Babylon's Nimrod and that the Astor family was known as the Astarte in Canaan. Blood is more important than surnames."

In the article The Astor Bloodline which I found on www.bibliotecapleyades.net it says that, "The Astors also have been very prominent in the 'Group' which is Britain's equivalent to the Skull & Bones Society. In Britain, the Astors, along with about 20 other families dominate the Group, just as certain families like the Whitneys in the U.S. help dominate the Order of Skull & Bones. Again, as was earlier pointed out, the key to understanding Satanism is the bloodlines."

The same article mentions that John Jacob Astor "married a Todd, a family frequently associated with Satanism."

I want to clarify that I am not making a generalized statement that encompasses every Freemason in this book as being evil and involved with the Occult.

However, in my research the elite society, who blashpeme and mock God, do so to fulfill an evil homage to their "fallen angel."

Make no mistake about it, the Freemasons that are in cahoots with the Illuminati are involved with Satan and this beckons me to forewarn all my readers that this life truly is a battle for you soul.
I hope you choose God!

9

THE THEORY OF RELATIVITY

The Theory of Relativity

Alexander Ray

In case you are not too familiar with the inner workings of space, relativity, and gravity, I have included some articles and key points for your analysis.

Some of it is very complex and technical but most of it, no matter how you analyze it, is theoretical! This goes back to my preface of the book, where I mentioned how the scientific dictators used one theory to explain another and another. All of these theories preconceived by observation and wild imagination.

Albert Einstein's theory of relativity postulates, that over time, the space that makes up the universe is expanding.

Wikipedia, says that at present, that "for all intents and purposes, it is safe to assume that the universe is infinite in spatial extent, without edge or strange connectedness."

But you see; this is exactly what I have been referring to the entire book, that the biased educators want you to believe!

If you believe the heliocentric model of earth and never question anything you will continue to believe that we are all an anomalous species out of millions of possibilities in the universe, therefore what we do in our everyday lives is futile and mundane. Aleister Crowley, the most famous Satan worshipper, states in his law to "Do what thou wilt." Instead of

thanking and praising our creator.

That is the reason that they want you to believe the dogma that humans are not important when compared to the millions and billions of other stars, suns and life that must exist in other worlds in the ever expanding cosmos.

This is why we need to question everything that we see, hear or read that involves NASA.

I want to now introduce a very lengthy, but intelligent article from the Universe Today website.

I actually found this at www.waykiwayki.com

The Mainstream version of Gravity

It states the following about The Theory of Relativity:

In our Solar System, not only does the Sun exert gravity on all the planets, keeping them in their orbits, but each planet exerts a force of gravity on the Sun, as well as all the other planets, too, all to varying degrees based on the mass and distance between the bodies. And it goes beyond just our Solar System, as actually, every object that has mass in the Universe attracts every other object that has mass—again, all to varying degrees based on mass and distance.

Schools and NASA teach that the 1000 mph spinning of the Earth, has nothing to do with gravity. Earth spins because it has always spun and there is no friction to slow it down. Basically, humans are taught that it is not the spin that keeps things stuck to the Earth. Universe today article quote.

The article also says that "this rotation is trying to spin you off into space, but don't worry, this force isn't much."

I am sorry, but 1000 miles per hour pretty fast, I mean 40 miles per hour on a boat is hauling butt!

Still the article states that "mainstream science says gravity is so strong that upside-down water at the surface of the ocean (near air) is being pulled to the center of the earth, but this force is also not strong enough in that this water, can move in any direction with currents and tides and be easily scooped, splashed, and thrown by a human hand."

"But this gravity force can bend water, so that is why

you can see the curve of earth which gives it the marble shape."

Continuing with this article, from Universe Today: "But this theory of gravity is not complete, the math is super complex, and no man on earth truly understands it."

I want to keep stressing some of the great points that this article touches on about gravity.

"Science claims our earth is surrounded by a giant vacuum of space and that we are moving through space at a speed of 514,000 miles per hour, yet the feeble pull of *gravity* on air holds it to our World. Turn on a vacuum and it sucks the air right into it. Why does Space not pull our air into it?" Universe Today article.

One non believer, of all this pseudo-science mumbo jumbo was Wilbur Voliva and he did not believe in the existence of the magical force called gravity. As such, he gave lectures all over America against Newtonian astronomy.

Sir Isaac Newton, formulated Newton's law of Gravitation in 1666. Once again with the "666."

I found a book *The Greatest Lie on Earth: Proof That Our World is Not a Moving Globe* by Edward Hendrie. It gives a lengthy quote by David Wardlow Scott that states the following about gravity:

Any object which is heavier than air and which is unsupported, has a natural tendency to fall by its own weight. Newton's famous apple at Woolsthorpe, or any other apple when ripe, loses hold of its stalk, and, being heavier than the air, drops as a matter of necessity, to the ground, totally irrespective of any attraction of the Earth. For, if such attraction existed, why does not the Earth attract the rising smoke which is not nearly so heavy as the apple? The answer is simple- because the smoke is lighter than the air, and, therefore, does not fall but ascends. Gravitation is only a subterfuge, employed by Newton in his attempt to prove that the Earth revolves round the Sun, and the quicker it is relegated to the tomb of all the Capulets, the better will it be for all classes of society. He draped his idol with the tawdry tinsel of false science, knowing well how to beguile the thoughtless multitude, for, with a littler alteration of Byron's famous lines, it is still true that '[m]ortals, like moths, are often caught by glare. And folly wins success where Seraphs might despair."-Gravitation is a clever illustration of the art of hocus-pocus- heads I win, tails you lose; Newton won his fame, and the people lost their senses. – David Wardlaw Scott, "Terra Firma."

This supposed law of gravitation, is often said to be an absolute truth and great discovery of science. How is it an absolute truth, where is the proof it exists?

Please continue reading some of this outstanding article, –Thomas Winship in Zetetic Cosmogeny (36) says that:

If, therefore, it can be shown that gravitation is a pure assumption, and an imagination of the mind only, that is has no existence outside of the brains of its expounders and advocates, the whole of the hypotheses of this modern so-called science fall to the ground as flat as the surface of the ocean," and this "most exact of all sciences," this wonderful "feat of the intellect" becomes at once the most ridiculous superstition and the most gigantic imposture to which ignorance and credulity could ever be exposed.

In closing this chapter, I want to capture this quote from the book by Hendrie, as it says on page 237:

"There is no such thing as gravity; gravity is not necessary on a flat earth. It is density that keeps objects from floating off the surface of the earth. People and objects are heavier than the air and therefore do not float off the ground. There are some gasses, of course, that are lighter than air, and they float off the ground. Everyone has seen helium balloons are not some sort of anti-gravity devices; they float up in the air, because helium is lighter than air. Why do people not understand that apples fall from trees to the ground, not because of gravity, but because apples are denser than air? They believe in the mystical force of gravity, not because it has been proven true, but because they have been brainwashed into believing in it. Gravity does not exist. David Wardlaw Scott.

THE BLUE MARBLE

The Blue Marble

Alexander Ray

Did you know that the very first picture of the whole earth, which is called, "The Blue Marble," was taken on December 7, 1972, by the crew of the Apollo 17 spacecraft, at a distance of about 28,000 miles away? I obtained this trivial information from Wikipedia. It is the most iconic picture and you probably have seen it in text books, films and movies.

100

However, I don't know if you knew this or not, but it is not
a real picture. It is a composite drawing and NASA admits
this.

You can go on Google and check for yourself.

The lunacy here is that NASA has changed this picture
of earth over the years.

Sometimes the United States of America looks extremely big, almost like an entire continent, and sometimes it looks smaller. Over the years the blue marble picture has changed, but has made NASA ever more courageous at releasing the fake photos of earth. For example, in one photo mosaic of earth, the word "Sex" is spelled upside down using clouds just to the left of between the north and south American continents. Please see picture on the right above.

It is very sick and perverted and it should be your duty as a truth seeker and educated person to investigate these liars!

In addition, clouds on the composite drawings can be seen to be cut and pasted throughout the drawing, making it easy to spot as a fake since clouds are the same size and same shape and are scattered haphazardly on the fake photo. The globe earth composite picture, changes colors also, and this shows that NASA can't make up their minds of which drawing or picture to post up as a real Earth picture.

Think about this, not one picture of earth had ever been seen until the fake space race and the fake space walk by Yuri Gagarin on April 12, 1961.

Throughout history humans did not possess the technology to go up high enough to encounter the invisible shield in the sky that separates the waters from the waters. So the shape of the earth was never questioned until this time and era in our history.

However, NASA admits that in order to produce the entire picture of the earth, they need image analyzing software to produce photo mosaics.

I found a sensational and impossible picture in an article in nasa.gov website. The caption in the picture reads "Earth as seen on July 6, 2015 from a distance of one million miles by a NASA scientific camera aboard the Deep Space Climate Observatory spacecraft." This is the picture on the right hand side above. The article continues with "The EPIC team now is working on a rendering of these images that emphasizes land features and removes this atmospheric effect."

NASA can't even take a real picture of the Earth, with a cell phone or a Canon 35 mm camera from the 200 mile low earth orbiting International Space Station, but we are supposed to believe this picture of Earth from one million miles away is real ?

"Doesn't this all sound like nonsense?"

There is also another mosaic photograph that has made its rounds on television, and movies and documentaries, etc. It is called the, "Black Marble", which is the nighttime view of Earth. According to Wikipedia, "The data was acquired by the Suomi NPP satellite in April and October 2012 and then mapped over existing Blue Marble imagery of Earth to provide a realistic view of the planet."

Why is this picture of Earth so important?

Well, it really is consummately important. This composite picture helped the propaganda and brainwashing machine that is NASA, promote their agenda of what the true shape of the earth looks like.

Remember the quote of Satan being the "Father of Lies?"

Once they got this picture perfected, they were able to put to rest the reality of the earth being flat with a firmament, by displaying a supposed "real photograph" of the earth and showing it as a round shaped ball. This had to be the case in order to continue the illusion that they went to outer space and captured the picture, and to prove that the earth is a globe. In effect, it validated everything that they had been teaching in history books as the truth.

By using illusions to prove that the Earth is a globe shape, since "a picture is worth a thousand words", they could prove all the teachings of the other Freemasons throughout history about the heliocentric earth model, and further separate God from our creation.

Please be forewarned about this clandestine and logistically planned demonic agenda!

This photograph of earth from space was exactly what NASA needed next as the final proof, in order to get the entire world onboard, and thereby, establishing NASA as the disseminator of science and "reality". With this fake mosaic of earth, NASA established themselves as the only entity in the world that had the technology to go into space and take this first and only grandiose picture of earth.

I wonder what thought crossed their minds when NASA realized that the Earth is the center of the universe?

The reality of it is that no rocket or space craft can breach the firmament. There is no Space X or real trips to Mars or any other planet. Planets are merely wandering stars or lights in the firmament just like the bible informs us.

Do you remember the illusions created by the very infamous Wizard of Oz; and it was all done with smoke and mirrors?

If all the pictures of earth are real, then why is one of NASA's own saying something different about the shape of the earth?

I found a video where Neil Degrasse Tyson says that Earth is an oblate spheroid and is fatter around the equator, than at the poles. So he says it is more of a pear shape! "What?" "Seriously?"

This was from a video from one of the most popular Flat Earth proponents, Eric Dubay. The video that I am referring to is entitled "Neil Degrasse Tyson Says Earth is Pear Shaped."

So then, what about the perfect "blue marble" pictures of the planet?

Neil Degrasse Tyson is an astrophysicist, cosmologist, author, and science communicator.

In an interview on "The Verge", there is a journalist that is interviewing Neil Degrasse Tyson, and the journalist, in reference to a new show involving him, asked about religion and how they adjust and "navigate the waters, of faith and science" on the show.

Mr. Tyson defends science by stating that they are offering science and telling stories about the past, and scientists or thinkers and the persecution that they encountered when they shared these views with the public. Of course he is referring to Galileo, Kepler, Copernicus and other heliocentric proponents. He wants the world to see these key players as martyrs and as innocent victims of a cruel world.

Ultimately, he says that "science will come to emergent truths about the universe versus dogma."

They are talking about a show called Cosmos. What is so ironic about the entire premise of the show, is that they begin the first episode of Cosmos, by following a Christian monk named Giordano Bruno who is persecuted during the Inquisition because his ideas were bigger than the ideas of the time.

In other words, (still discussing the show Cosmos), Bruno believed that if the sun was a star, like the millions of other stars in the night sky, then these stars must have planets, and if they have planets, then they might have life.

Strange coincidence here of art imitating life, or Pseudo-scientists and cosmologists postulating that there are millions of other galaxies and stars and planets.

Bruno is the hero in Cosmos, and he gets killed by the people that believed the God model; that Earth is the center of the solar system.

I find this so interesting to know, that Cosmos: A Spacetime Odyssey (TV mini-series) is a documentary series that explores how we discovered the laws of nature and found our bearings in space and time, and you guessed it, Neil Degrasse Tyson is the host.

Once again, they are using propaganda any which way possible to sustain the "Masonic Induced Hypnosis" to explain the universe and the illusion of the world which they created from the 1931 Big Bang hypothesis.

Revelations 22:13 (KJV) "I am Alpha and the Omega, the first and the last, the beginning and the end."

These words from our Creator have existed way longer than the Big Bang Theory!

11

GENESIS AND THE FIRMAMENT

Genesis and the Firmament

Alexander Ray

Although I have always been a Catholic, albeit, not a practicing one, writing this book extemporaneously allowed me to embrace my faith, and it also allowed me to dedicate my life to becoming a more devout Catholic. Amen!

Who knows, maybe I see myself writing a series of books on all the subject matter in this book.

All I really care about it to expose the truth, whether that is talking about it, blogging about it, or writing about it or uploading videos on YouTube in the future.

Throughout all my research, I ended up researching the Bible and the story of Creation. The Bible really gave me the best resource for the true shape of the earth, since it is a Divine inspirational book, and it contains all the information that I needed for this book or for any research.

I do not think that any true Flat Earth investigator can refrain from referencing the Bible in order to defend our principles and beliefs.

In the book of Genesis, in the Old Testament of the King James Version, it starts with the following:

1 "In the beginning, God created the heaven and the earth." (KJV)

According to science, the creation of the universe needed three essential things and that is time, space, and matter in order to exist and form. Well here it is in black and white, time..."In the beginning," space..."heaven" and matter...."the earth." I am in no way taking credit, for this idea, I did read it somewhere in my research.

2 "And the earth was without form, and void; and darkness was upon the face of the deep.

And the Spirit of God moved upon the face of the waters." (KJV)

"In the Bible the Spirit always signifies life. What is the significance of the waste, void, darkness, and deep water?

All these signify a disaster, and even death. These are all negative things. Then all of a sudden something good came, that is the Spirit." I got this information from L. Witness, in "The History of God in His Union with Man."

Many experts and scientists, have speculated the age of the earth to be 4 billion years old. No one really knows the age of the Earth only God. One person one day woke up and looked at the different strata in rock and decided that each one layer represented millions of years of erosion and weather related phenomena, and that is how one rock formation formed on top of other formation over millions of years. He hypothesized this and other geologists agreed and then science strikes again!

However, I really do not believe that dinosaurs roamed the earth. If this is the case, then I do not believe in fossils or fossil fuel for that matter. I know I introduced it in the beginning of my book, however, I did not want to explain too much, in the first few pages of the book. Please check out a video by Eric Dubay entitled "The Atlantean Conspiracy: Dinosaurs Hoax – Dinosaurs Never Existed."

What I do believe is that somehow, when the face or Spirit of our Almighty God, moved through the Earth, this is when oil was deposited into the Earth. Moreover, this may have been how God embedded all the other resources like carbon, silver, gold, aluminum, titanium, and all the other elements of the Periodic Table. He masterfully designed this knowing the value of the different physical and chemical properties that each element would provide for mankind to survive and prosper in his Earth. This is another reason why I dispute the Big Bang Theory of the Universe. Of course, this is just my own belief.

But to all those hard pressed ball earth proponents out there, let us forget about the Biblical Earth, for a minute, and subscribe to the aforementioned theory. Let us assume that every circumstance and random cosmic chance did happen to spark the Big Bang and we derived from a primordial soup.

How did all these elements from the Periodic table, wind up on Earth and not on the moon or any other planet to sustain life as we know it?

Not only this, we needed a planet with a vast amount of H_2O. You know the earth is covered by more water than mass right? I mean the waters are somehow connected from the ocean waters to the waters of the deep. Whatever oscillates down there, makes the tides in our oceans. Thomas Winship thought that "Tides are caused by the gentle and gradual rise and fall of the earth on the bosom of the might deep." He stated this in his "Zetetic Cosmogeny." Page 130-131.

We all know that water is known as the "Universal Solvent," right?

Most liquids used today, and even our human body is comprised of 50-65% water. We use water to drink and bathe, brush our teeth, wash clothes. We can't survive without drinking water for more than 3-4 days. We use water to mix chemicals in order to create the products that we use in society. The Earth has everything that we need to have allowed humans to thrive on Earth for so long. Every tree and every seed that is planted brings forth fruit and vegetables and some even emit oil. Cotton for example, changed our lives for the better, minus slavery of course, by allowing us to have any fabric that we use including the clothes that we wear, and we get it from a plant.

Photosynthesis is a process used by plants and other organisms to convert light energy, normally form the Sun, into chemical energy that can be later released to fuel the organisms' activities. I got this information from Wikipedia. In addition, plants provide Carbon dioxide and also emit molecular oxygen. Humans, of course then breath in oxygen from the air. It is spread out throughout the body via the blood stream. Then we expel the carbon dioxide through our lungs.

Another major resource which I read that is being extracted from the oceans since we almost run out of is sand. Do you know the value of sand on this Earth? Well, we use it as a major compound or ingredient to make concrete. When it is mixed with cement and water, it solidifies and makes the concrete that we use to make buildings, highways, and our homes. Sand is also used in the micro chips used to make computers. Sand has many more uses, and you can read about it more on Google.

I am sure there are thousands of more examples that

seem to indicate that Genesis is the conclusive blueprint of how all this world came into being. This sounds like a very intricate and divine master plan from an Omnipotent designer.

Just ponder the greatness that is the human spinal cord. It is a very complex and intricate component that makes up part of our central nervous system. The brain is the other part.

How did our human body's anatomy become so complex from a single cell organism? How?

Nobody knows how much time passed before God moved forward with his Creation. In other words, some people say the earth was literally created in 7 days like the bible says. Still, others say the earth is billions of years old.

Cosmologists say that time didn't exist until the Big Bang. They have two models that they use, along with quantum mechanics and physics to hypothesize theories of what may have happened to spark the Big Bang.

They do admit though that "this rapidly expanding universe was pretty much empty of matter, but it harbored huge amounts of dark energy, the theory goes....During inflation, dark energy made the universe smooth out and accelerate. But it didn't stick around for long.It was just temporary dark energy. It converted into ordinary matter and radiation through a process called reheating. The universe went from being cold during inflation to being hot again when all the dark energy went away." Scientists don't know what might have spurred inflation. That remains one of the key questions in Big Bang cosmology, Fillipenko said,"according to the author M. Wall in *The Big Bang: What Really Happened at Our Universe's Birth?*"

Alex Fillipenko is an astrophysicist of the University of California, Berkeley.

Please, let us continue with Genesis.

3 "And God said, Let there be light: and there was light." (KJV)

4 "And God saw the light, that it was good: and God divided the light from the darkness." (KJV)

5 "And God called the light Day, and the darkness he called Night. And the evening and the morning were the first day." (KJV)

6 "And God said, Let there be a *firmament* in the midst of the waters, and let it divide the waters from the waters." (KJV)

This is the firmament that I have been referring to in the book. It is like a dome that surrounds the upper half of the earth on the flat plane that we live in.

7 "And God made the firmament, and divided the waters which were under the firmament from the waters which were above the firmament: and it was so." (KJV)

8 "And God called the firmament Heaven. And the evening and the morning were the second day." (KJV)

14 "And God said, Let there be lights in the firmament of the heaven to divide the day from the night, and let them be for signs, and for seasons, and for days and years." (KJV)

Right here is where we get all the ancient models of our earth, like the heliocentric, the geocentric and even hybrids of the two. Astronomers, as well as scientists and observers before the telescope was invented, looked up to the sky and recorded their observations of the stars, the moon and all the planets.

Which model you choose to believe is up to you, except only one model can be true and the "Biblical Earth" is right.

As God commanded, humans were able to create accurate calendars and time keeping clocks and almanacs which helps us keep track of time. After all, it is important to know what day and month we are in and to track important life changing events.

15 "And let them be for lights in the firmament of the heaven to give light upon the earth: and it was so." (KJV)

16 "And God made two great lights; the greater light to rule the day, and the lesser light to rule the night; he made the stars also." (KJV)

17 "And God set them in the firmament of the heaven to give light upon the earth." (KJV)

Think about this statement here, "God set them in the firmament of the heaven to give light upon the earth" so I believe this is where the sun and the moon are located in and there is no way that the sun is 98 million miles away and that the moon is some 245,000 miles from earth. According to Flat Earth research, both the Sun and the

Moon are the same size and they are 3000 miles away. One researcher of the flat earth stated recently that a laser test that measures distance was used and the moon showed to be about 100 miles away. Nobody really knows the answer to the distance, but I do not believe NASA.

Another quote from the bible about the firmament follows here:

In Job 37:18 (KJV) it says the following about the firmament, "Hast thou with him spread out the sky, which is strong, an as a molten looking glass?"

Earth would be more easily defined as a system environment. Earth is also a machine, it is a Tesla coil. The sun and the moon are powered wirelessly with the electromagnetic field (the Aether). This field also suspends the celestial spheres with electromag[netic] levitation. Electromag[netic] levitation disproves gravity because the only force you need to counter is the electromagnetic force, not gravity. The stars are attached to the firmament.

–   Nikola Tesla

Some strong proof of the firmament comes from two very reputable and respected Universities and it comes from a study called *Did Scientists Discover the Firmament?* In this recent study from the Massachusetts Institute of Technology and the University of Colorado Boulder the study concluded and found that the Earth is indeed guarded from fast moving electrons. Daniel Baker, the lead author of the study concluded that this invisible shield is about 7200 miles above the Earth. Furthermore, in an article entitled "Star Trek-like invisible shield found thousands of miles above Earth", Baker states that "It's almost like this electrons are running into a glass wall in space. Somewhat like the shields created by force fields on Star Trek that were used to repel alien weapons, we are seeing an invisible shield blocking these electrons. It's an extremely puzzling phenomenon."

The harmful, damaging electrons make up the outer band of the Van Allen radiation belt and these electrons can harm electronics, and pose serious health risks to humans, and we have covered this when I discussed project Orion.

Thanks to the firmament, and thanks to God, the electrons cannot come into the Earth's atmosphere, the firmament is like an invisible force field. I really think that our entire solar system and planet exists with one phenomena that is measureable and demonstrable and that is electricity. Electromagnetism, magnetism, frequency, oscillation, all relate to electricity directly or indirectly and I believe Nicola Tesla knew this and he stated once that " If you want to find the secrets of the universe, think in terms of energy, frequency and vibration."

I would like to continue quoting from Genesis.

18 "And to rule over the day and over the night, and to divide the light from the darkness: and God saw that it was good." (KJV)

19 "And the evening and the morning were the fourth day." (KJV)

20 "And God said, Let the waters bring forth abundantly the moving creature that hath life, and fowl that may fly above the earth in the open firmament of heaven." (KJV)

21 "And God created great whales, and every living creature that moveth, which the waters brought forth abundantly, after their kind, and every winged fowl after his kind: and God saw that it was good." (KJV)

22 "And God blessed them, saying, Be fruitful and multiply, and fill the waters in the seas, and let fowl multiply in the earth." (KJV)

Why else do you think that new living creatures are being discovered to this day? I mean how many times, do you remember picking up a newspaper, or opening up Google and reading a story about a new species of fish, or bird, or insect, that was discovered?

23 "And the evening and the morning were the fifth day." (KJV)

24 "And God said, Let the earth bring forth the living creature after his kind, cattle, and creeping things, and beast of the earth after his kind; and it was so." (KJV)

25 "And God made the beast of the earth after his kind, and cattle after their kind, and every thing that creepeth upon the earth after his kind: and God saw that it was good." (KJV)

I underlined the words "his kind" here in order to

explain something; another heart felt intuition. I believe that "his kind," means that evolution cannot be true, since one animal, when procreating creates the same animal of its own "kind". In other words, one species does not "evolve" into another. A cow gives birth to a cow, a horse gives birth to a horse, and a human gives birth to a human, and so forth. Just as God commanded.

26 "And God said, Let us make man in our image, after our likeness: and let them have dominion over the fish of the sea, and over the fowl of the air and over the cattle, and over all the earth, and over every creeping thing that creepeth upon the earth." (KJV)

This commandment by God establishes mankind to have dominion over all the Earth and every living creature in it.

27 "So God created man in his own image, in the image of God created he him; male and female created he them." (KJV)

28 "And God blessed them, and God said unto them, Be fruitful, and multiply, and replenish the earth, and subdue it; and have dominion over the fish of the sea, and over the fowl of the air, and over every living thing that moveth upon the earth" (KJV).

29 "And God said, Behold, I have given you every herb bearing seed, which is upon the face of all the earth, and every tree, in the which is the fruit of a tree yielding seed; to you it shall be for meat." (KJV)

30 "And to every beast of the earth, and to every fowl

of the air, and to every thing that creepeth upon the earth, wherein there is life, I have given every green herb for meat: and it was so." (KJV)

31 "And God saw every thing that he made, and, behold, it was very good. And the evening and the morning were the sixth day." (KJV)

In Genesis chapter 2 God rests.

2:2 "And on the seventh day God ended his work which he had made; and he rested from all his work which he had made." (KJV)

In Chronicles 16:30, KJV it says to "Fear before him, all the earth: the world also shall be stable, that it be not moved."

This passage of the bible makes me strongly believe that the Earth really does sit on pillars.

Here we see that if this is so, then how can the earth, be a spinning ball tilted on its 23.4 degrees from 90 degrees. The difference leaves the number 66.6.

Coincidence? No, I don't think so. It is another way that the Freemasons and elite mock the feeble minded believers.

Finally in Isaiah 45:18 (ESV) "For thus says the Lord, who created the heavens (he is God!), who formed the earth and made it (he established it; he did not create it empty, he formed it to be inhabited!): I am the Lord, and there is no other."

Stephen Hawking, however, has something different to say about creation. He says, and I quote, "Time didn't exist before the Big Bang, so there is no time for God to make the universe in. It's like asking for directions to the edge of the Earth. The Earth is a sphere. It does not have an edge, so looking for it is a futile exercise." He stated this in the following article aptly called "*Stephen Hawking: God Could not Create the Universe Because There Was No Time for Him to Do So.*

I think that deception has been ongoing since biblical times. For example, in the book of Exodus, the Pharaoh and his group of magicians had people believing that Pharaoh commanded the sun to rise every morning, and also that the Pharaoh commanded eclipses to occur. Currently, we should call these magicians, scientists.

12

ANTARCTICA - THE OUTER EDGE

Antarctica- The Outer Edge

Alexander Ray

This part of the book deals with Antarctica and will paint a better picture, hopefully, of the postulated true boundaries of the enigmatic Earth that we all live in.

In my research, it turns out that Antarctica actually surrounds the entire Earth and is indeed the edge of the world. Just imagine a huge ring of ice that surrounds the Earth and holds the oceans' waters. Therefore, Antarctica

---

is not in the South Pole nor is it a small continent as Wikipedia states.

Antarctica supposedly is about twice the size of Australia according to Wikipedia.

This is where the culmination of all the research and experiments and reports have added to the truth of a Flat Earth. It started back with Captain James Cook a British Naval Captain in the Royal Navy. According to Wikipedia, in three voyages around the globe he sailed thousands of miles. In his ever courageous spirit he attempted to circumnavigate Antarctica. His voyage took 3 to 4 years and he traveled over 50,000 miles. He is credited with discovering Australia, and New Zealand.

I am so excited to write this chapter, because of the evidence that is written, and posted in videos, and interviews and in history books.

For example, there is a great video online on YouTube where "YouWhatMate?" shows a 5 minutes and 6 second video where he plots the 2nd voyage of Captain Cook when he left Britain. It really makes sense on a Flat Earth and the outer edge being Antarctica and the Ice Wall making his voyage last almost 3 years in order to try and find a way through. However, he literally was only going in circles, "One big circle that is!"

The video is entitled "Captain Cook; Antarctic Journey Proves Flat Earth."

Another discovery, so you can envision the magnitude and sheer awesomeness of the sight of what explorers have set their eyes on when they reach the edge of the earth, is found on an excerpt from Captain Cook himself.

In a magazine journal called Scientific American: Supplement, Volume 48 No. 1258 I found an article that has excerpts from Captain Cook where he was not able to penetrate the supposed Antarctic continent. Here is the excerpt for you to read:

Four hours later he was stopped by a great ice barrier in latitude 71 degrees south, where the mountains of ice, rising one above the other, tier upon tier, into the distance were lost in the clouds of the polar sky. The desolate grandeur of that icy coast appalled the great navigator, and, seeing no possibility of pushing to the pole over those impassable mountains, he contended himself with having gone further than any one had ever been before, and, he thought as far as any man could go."

In the same article, Sir James Ross also witnessed the view and "from the coast line, where the walls of ice stood as sheer cliffs hundreds of feet high, the mountains in land ranged one over the other, culminating in the volcanic peaks 12,000 feet high."

Another informative video that really made me wonder and contemplate about the edge of the world is a video on YouTube where they interview an avid explorer and Freemason Admiral by the name of Richard E. Byrd.

It is the Longines Chronoscope, a television journal, where a CBS correspondent and a National Affair editor are conducting an interview of the reputable Admiral

Richard E. Byrd. Larry Laseur, CBS correspondent asks
Admiral Bird, if there is a difference between the top of
the world and the bottom of the world. To which Admiral
Byrd answers with the following reply:

There is, now the North Pole is the sum of an ocean
10,000 feet deep. The South Pole is a sum of a plateau
10,000 feet high- the North Pole is sea-surrounded by
continents slightly frozen. The Antarctic continent is
surrounded by a belt of ice of at least 1200 miles. [It is]
surrounded by seas frozen at least 1200 miles thick. Now
the south is a plateau, it gets in some places 14,000 feet
up. I've been over in areas of 15,000 feet and it's a little bit
chilly up there. So there's that big difference between the
top and bottom of the world.

Still another brave explorer that went to the edge to
explore Antarctica was General A.W. Greely, and he
wrote the following: The ice-barrier, so frequently
referred to in accounts of the Antarctic regions, is the
fore-front of the enormous glacier-covering, of ice-cap,
which, accumulating in vast, undulating fields from the
heavy snowfall, and ultimately attaining hundreds, if not
thousands, of feed in thickness, creeps form the continent
of Antarctica into the polar sea. The ice-barrier, yet a part
of the parent ice-cap, presents itself to the navigator who
has boldness enough to approach its fearful front, as a
solid, perpendicular wall of marble-like ice, ranging from
one thousand to two thousand feet in thickness, of which

from one hundred to two hundred feet sinks below, the level of the sea.

Upon his return from this famous expedition, Admiral Byrd admitted his findings and in his expert opinion he suspected that the United States government as well as many other nations would mount expeditions year after year and that there was nobody living there. He called this place the most valuable important place for science. He also added that "there was an untouched reservoir, for military importance that had at least something like 180 miles, with enough coal, and evidence of other valuable resources. He said that the area he was describing was about the size of the United States and that it could have been once tropical there and thought that there may be oil. He mentioned another raw mineral, uranium in this region. Admiral Byrd added that countries like Russia, Australia, Argentina, New Zealand, Chile and Great Britain were very interested in launching expeditions. He stated that it was a very peaceful place, but he did not believe that it would remain this way."

Maybe what Admiral Byrd discovered is more land on Earth, land that is not mapped or plotted on any map of earth. We can only wonder and speculate what he really discovered. I guess we will never really know the truth.

Admiral Byrd suspected that much like the discovery of America, or the gold rush in California, back in the day, Antarctica would quickly become populated with many opportunistic countries needing resources that were discovered there.

But, to the admiral's surprise, all these countries whose scientists were exploring there, signed the Antarctic Treaty in Washington in 1959. It was about 12 countries, according to Google.

The treaty was an international agreement and the gathering of all these nations agreed that Antarctica was to be used for peaceful purposes only. 47 Nations are in agreement with regulating tourism. I read somewhere that the environmental protection acts that became so stringent in Antarctica came much later.

So my question is, "What exactly did these countries find in Antarctica?" The protection of the environment was not the priority at the time of whatever discovery they made in Antarctica.

Whatever they did find, it is still uncanny that they adopted the flag or insignia that closely resembles the flat earth map.

The United States with its technology and resources did express interest in going to Antarctica. In referencing *Operation High Jump; Journey to Antarctica to Find the Dome*, a planetruth tells us the following:

Immediately after WWII the U.S. Navy rushed launched the largest military operation ever down to

Antarctica called Operation High Jump. Admiral Byrd, a 33 degree Freemason led the expedition of 30 ships and 4700 militarized soldiers. The mission had 3 task forces that were sent out in different directions and was to last 6-8 months but the fleet came back in just 6 weeks. Admiral Byrd reported UFO sightings, but that was a public relations ruse, they were really trying to find out about the electromagnetic field which is the firmament above the ice wall and the edge of the dome.

Just several years later the U.S. and the Russians began firing over 49 high altitude thermos nuclear rockets up into the dome with Operation Fishbowl and Dominic.

Don't even try to use Google maps to study the supposed continent of Antarctica since you will get a fake image of a white blurry CGI image that is supposedly the continent of Antarctica. You won't be able to see any details whatsoever from the aerial view, like you can any other place of the Earth.

While you are exploring Google maps, you should go to Devon Island, (the largest uninhabited island on Earth) in Canada and you may see the topography and the rover that looks exactly like the pictures that are coming from Mars.

I would like to now share a passage from the Bible that reinforces the flat earth, and it comes from Isaiah 40:21-22:

40:21 "Have ye not known? Have ye not heard? Hath it not been told you from the beginning? Have ye not understood from the foundations of the earth?

40:22 "It is he that sitteth upon the circle of the earth, and the inhabitants thereof are as grasshoppers; that stretcheth out the heavens as a curtain, and spreadeth them out as a tent to dwell in."

Here it is easy to misconstrue circle, with ball or something else, especially when they translated the bible into our English language.

I wonder if maybe the prophet Isaiah, misspoke.

However, as truth Seeker a.k.a. as Sola Scriptura, points out in their video on YouTube entitled, "Flat Earth: Want the truth?" in Isaiah 22:18 (KJV) "He will surely violently turn and toss thee like a ball into a large country..."

In these passages, we can clearly tell that Isaiah, knew exactly the difference between the words, "ball" and "circle."

Clearly, the prophet chose his words correctly and it is logical to see the Earth from above as a flat circle.

In order to continue to draw what the Earth may look like I want to add some research from Wilbur Glenn Voliva. As a side note, his last name and my true last name, have the same five letters.

Wilbur Glenn Voliva, whom I mentioned back in the beginning chapters of this book, offered $5000 dollars to anyone that could prove that the earth was a sphere, floating in space.

"Voliva's conception of a flat world, with the North Pole in the center and the sun revolving in its orbit above the equator. A wall of ice around the edge of the earth keeps adventurous mariners from falling off into space," according to aplanetuth in "Plane not a Planet."

For example, in Job 26:7 from the Old Testament, Chapter 26 verse 7 in English Standard Version, "He stretches out the north over the void and hangs the earth on nothing."

So in other words, we really do not have a real photograph of what our enigmatic Earth looks like.

Still, some more deceptions, and made up illustrations, from the elite, include stars.

However, I am not going into depth about what stars are, or about their physical composition.

In Universe today, in an article by Cain, F. (12 Feb, 2009) *Size of Stars* it says that "The smallest stars out there are the tiny red dwarfs. These are stars with no more than 50% the mass of the Sun, and they can have as little as 7.5% the mass of the Sun. One fairly well know example of a red dwarf star is Proxima Centauri; the closest star to Earth. This star has about 12% the mass of the Sun, and about 14% the size of the Sun- about 200,km across, which is only a little larger than Jupiter."

More deception and more lies.

I want to present a verse from the book of Revelation 6:12-14 (KJV) "And I beheld when he had opened the sixth seal, and, lo, there was a great earthquake; and the sun became black as sackcloth of hair, and the moon became as blood; And the stars of heaven fell unto the earth, even as a fig tree casteth her untimely figs, when she is shaken of a mighty wind."

Now, how can one star be as big as Academia is telling us it is? I mean if this were the case, then one small tiny star should destroy our planet if it were to fall towards earth, right?

The bible, clearly portrays stars to be much smaller than the earth, since in Revelation the divine prophet uses the plural for "stars". Stars are said to be falling onto earth; please note here, the word, "falling' vs "hurling' to the earth.

I want to reiterate, my statement earlier in the book about the older religions believing in the Flat Earth model.

Some theologians speculate that some of the writers of the Old Testament had a Babylonian world view, which portrays the earth as flat and resting of pillars, and covered by a solid sky-dome (the Firmament).

Psalm 19 states that "The heavens declare the glory of God; and the firmament sheweth his handywork.

13

THE INTERNATIONAL SPACE STATION

The Internation Space Station

Alexander Ray

This chapter deals with the space shuttle and International Space Station and some astonishing findings. There is so much material to cover, that this chapter alone could become an entire book. Hmmm, maybe, later on down the road for me. Brevity aside, I do hope that you will connect the dots by now, into seeing how everything involving space and NASA needs to be second guessed and questioned further.

Firstly, to begin I would like to give you some of Wikipedia's information about the Space Shuttle. It says that the space shuttle was a partially reusable low Earth orbital spacecraft system operated by the U.S. National Aeronautics and Space Administration (NASA). In addition, some of the 135 missions that the space shuttles flew in, included the Hubble Space Telescope and participated in construction and servicing of the International Space Station.

The space shuttle was retired from service upon the end of Atlantis's final flight on July 21, 2011, and I got all this information from Wikipedia.

According to an article "Horrifying Fact You Didn't Know About the Space Shuttle" written by Pinchefsky C. in Forbes.com "The Shuttle had an operational altitude of only 120 to 600 miles. However, the Shuttle's trip to the ISS was only a 200-250 mile journey, approximately the distance between NYC and Boston. The Shuttle also flew to the Hubble Telescope, which is maintained at an altitude of 350 miles, a little less than the distance from NYC to Norfolk, VA."

Really quickly here, if you ask me, if I believe that there is an orbiting Hubble Space Telescope around Earth, I say this to NASA and all the Flat Earth debunkers out there:

"Snap a real picture of the Earth with a cell phone or a digital camera from the ISS or from the Hubble Telescope, without, all the stuff about ultraviolet wavelength points, and, that will quiet the skeptics!"

If amateur rockets have gone further than 65 miles in altitude which is the threshold to "Space," and shot video of the earth and it appears to be stationary and flat, then NASA can snap a real photograph, right? Right.

What is wrong with seeing the ring of ice that surrounds the Earth?

In my opinion, I think that the images or photos that are purported to be taken by the Hubble telescope are obtained from the ground based observatories.

Another interesting investigation that I found was from a gentleman stating that the Space Shuttles are not gliders at all but are nothing more than a sophisticated jet airplane.

There is an active YouTube subscriber named "Russianvids" and he says that the chaser planes that escort the Space Shuttle when it comes back from space, are used to detract attention from the jet engine noise of the Space Shuttle itself.

Russianvids, does an amazing job in one of his videos entitled "NASA Space Shuttle Program Exposed-Space Shuttles Can't Breach God's Firmament.

The importance here, is that NASA says that the Space Shuttle acts like a glider only when landing. However, clearly they act more like a jet airplane. Now, this is important since a jet engine will not work in the vacuum of space.

In this video you can watch 2 or 3 space shuttle landings

where you can clearly hear the jet engine high pitched noise as the shuttle comes in to land.

Another great observation that "Rusianvids" catches about the Space Shuttle is the flimsy shocks that are supposed to hold the shuttle when it rides on top of an airplane when the shuttle is flown back to the home base.

He shows that if the weight of said shuttle is about 30 tons, how can these cheap looking fabricated angle irons hold such massive heavy space craft secure, to the airplane that it is riding piggy back on?

I would love to find out,what is actually up in space that is supposed to be the International Space Station?

The space station is said to be about the size of a football field.

Google says the dimensions are about 356 feet by 240 feet and weigh around 450 tons.

From the NASA website, to give you some more insight of the size of it, "the ISS is larger than a six bedroom house. ISS has an internal pressurized volume of 32,333 cubic feet, or equal that of a Boeing 747." This is according to Mark Garcia and Brian Dunbar from NASA website.

Also, an amazing fact that they want us to believe is that the ISS goes so fast that it could technically go round trip to the moon in one day. Also, according to NASA there are 52 computers controlling the ISS.

The ISS is orbiting around the earth and traveling at 17,164 miles per hour, at 253 miles above earth in Low Earth Orbit/ LEO.

However, staying true to my book, the ISS is a hoax just like anything concocted by NASA. I am not sure how they are accomplishing the computer program that tracks the ISS. I need to do further research, but I know that the truth will prevail.

There's a great website where you can go to check out for yourself, the fakery that is brought to you by NASA, and that is www.timetounite.com

In his article entitled "ISS Hoax-The International Space Station Does Not Exist!" Kiel, does an excellent job explaining the various tricks that NASA uses to pull off the "illusion" when they show interviews or pictures of astronauts floating around in the ISS.

Kiel, and many other researchers and ISS non-believers show videos of the special effects, models, pool, zero G planes that NASA uses to trick us.

In addition, various camera tricks, including green screen and CGI/ Computer Graphic Images in the background of still photos are used to create the "illusion" that the astronaut is standing inside the ISS. However, you can catch objects that do not seem to move which should be moving, for example computer or data cables in the background.

More evidence that suggests that NASA is lying to us about the ISS, is video of a few female astronauts on the ISS. These females, (Sunita Williams is one of these females) are usually wearing permed hair, this keeps their hair fixated in relationship to their head. They do this to give the "illusion" that their hair is actually being pulled up by being in zero gravity environment. However, if the female actually does a flip, and her head is facing downward, you can see that the hair doesn't bounce or move whatsoever. It really makes the hair with their perm look ridiculous!

Something else that I found that is very interesting about the space program is where our astronauts train for space walks.

The United States uses the NBL, or Neutral Buoyancy Lab training facility in Houston Texas which is a big swimming pool with the ISS.

And I believe that this is how NASA shoots spacewalks. In an interview that I saw, one astronaut said that everything inside the pool looks the same as the ISS, and so it is easy to connect the dots and speculate and wonder if this is the true ISS that they use in all their videos.

How else do you explain the air bubbles in so many videos of supposed ISS space walks?

Star City is a city in Russia, and it is located deep in a forest about 30 miles from Moscow. This is where cosmonauts have trained for 50 years and this is where the space walks take place.

In other videos of ISS, you can actually see air bubbles escaping from an astronaut's face shield and helmet.

In yet another picture of the ISS, you can actually see a diver with a scuba tank in one of the compartment of the ISS.

How can this be? The only logical explanation to capture an air bubble or air bubbles coming from anywhere, is if the astronauts are faking that they are in space, when in reality they are in water inside of a big swimming pool that is mocked up with green screens to project Computer Graphics Images of the Earth or whatever else they fabricate.

Also, there was an astronaut that almost drowned in space, recently, when a gallon of water mysteriously entered his face piece. Now, astronauts use an emergency snorkel to avert this from happening. You can research this in NASA's website.

In another video, I saw another air bubble coming from a Chinese astronaut's helmet. Then you can see the studio lights reflecting on the rectangular mirror wrist band that the Chinese astronaut was wearing on his spacewalk in the same video. Once again, the studio lights that are seen reflecting have to be what is used to illuminate the mock up space station where they are creating the illusion that they are doing spacewalks.

I would like to reference Genesis 1:6 (KJV) "And God said, Let there be a firmament in the midst of the waters, and let it divide the waters from the waters."

Could it be possible that if the ISS does exist that it actually travels in some inexplicable physical state of "water"?

The astronauts really make it look very believable by

obtaining weightlessness which NASA says is a phenomenon of being in the vacuum of space.

Now, I would like to explain to you how the astronauts achieve weightlessness up in the International Fake Station.

A parabolic flight path which is done by a reduced-gravity aircraft is a type of fixed-wing aircraft that provides brief near-weightless environments, according to Wikipedia.

This aircraft is used for training astronauts in zero-g maneuvers, giving them about 25 seconds to 45 seconds of weightlessness out of 65 seconds of flight in each parabola. Basically, without getting all technical, the pilot manipulates the aircraft into a parabola flight path, i.e. up and down vector trajectory by pointing the nose of the airplane and manipulating the controls, and elevators of the aircraft. This in essence makes astronauts free-fall inside the aircraft.

NASA, may indeed have a mockup of the inside of the ISS inside of one or more of these big jet air planes where parabolic flights and videos are shot to later show to the media and the public as "live" coverage from inside the ISS during interviews with astronauts.

As I am typing these lines, I just had an epiphany! What if the reason that NASA chose the tubular design for the ISS, was to easily have mock up jet airplanes (which also are tubular shape inside) and then build different mock ups of the ISS on different planes.

Then they could use those different planes when the astronauts stand in front of the green screen to fake whatever they wish to do and say that they are onboard the ISS?

Genius!

Chris Hatfield is one of the astronauts that comes up in this video documentary. You can definitely see what looks like a harness under his red shirt that he wears in the video that I am referencing, and you can almost envision the wires that have been cropped out in order to hide the harness that is clearly holding him up. He inadvertently bends over to pick up an item, and that is when the deception is exposed.

Also, you can hear the noise of the airplane's jet engines, when they do extended ISS scenes. Why would you even be able to hear a loud jet engines on the ISS, unless they really are on an airplane and doing parabolic flight to simulate zero gravity. This fact was astutely found by Steve Blakey in his outstanding documentary video called "*ISS Space Station hoax yes the ISS and pretty much everything else to do with NASA.*"

Many other curious aspects of the ISS that Steve Blakey presents is all the questions that arise from having these astronauts essentially living in a high tech tin can, as he says. For example, in your home all the dust that accumulates over a period of a few days is mostly dead skin that dies off and creates dust. How do the astronauts clean or vacuum this dust or keep it from getting into the electronics or the supposed 50 computers that keep it flying? It is obvious that water would certainly damage the electronics onboard and if you open any water soluble bottle or spray, with zero gravity, the aerosol would go everywhere or would be very disruptive and difficult to contain.

In one interview with an astronaut in the ISS, he stated that when they brush their teeth, he has to spit the toothpaste into a rag, since gargling with water would be somewhat challenging and dangerous to the electronics onboard.

In another video posted by FuxNews entitled "International Space Station Hoax Analysis of Video Proves We're Being Lied to," Cady Coleman one of the astronauts on board the ISS, actually says in her interview that they swallow the toothpaste. However, later on she is seen playing with a big water bubble that is suspended in front of her face and then she swipes the remaining drops of water after she swallows most of the big bubble of water into her mouth. She haphazardly, swipes a few drops of water towards a laptop that is next to her.

The most definitive proof of trickery comes when Cady Coleman is being interviewed and she starts floating uncontrollably sideways. She tries to keep her composure, being the trooper that she is, but to no avail.

All these inconsistencies and awkward predicaments should make anyone question the authenticity of an actual ISS in space.

Another concern that Mr. Blakey asks involves the daily activity onboard the ISS. For example, living and breathing and drinking water and getting rid of their feces and urine and doing laundry, is no joke when it comes to contemplating how this is all accomplished up there 250 miles in orbit.

Chris Hatfield, in an interview on Conan O'Brian said that they dump their used laundry into a capsule and jettison overboard this capsule with their dirty laundry, and then it supposedly burns up upon re-entry into earth's atmosphere.

I found a video on YouTube that shows some pretty realistic views of the ISS and the space shuttle and the Earth. However, some scenes in the video do look fake. I am talking about "Space Shuttle STS-112 Atlantis Space Station Assembly ISS-9AS1 Truss 2002 NASA." It was posted by Jeff Quitney.

At 6:00 minutes into the video, of the 18 minute and 18 second video, the astronaut that is documenting the video, states that the following: "but before [the spacewalk] we always indulge in a few Pagan rights to apiece the EVA Gods. These little ceremonies are very, very, important to ensure mission success, if you do them right." Right after this statement you can see the four astronauts in the video break into a song and dance, and then throw the "Devil horn sign" with both hands. Two of the astronauts were helping the other two astronauts suit up to do the space walk. I just thought that this was worth mentioning and I thought that this was a very bizarre ritual.

The disingenuous footage in the video appear at the following time stamps:

3:11,3:18,3:36,5:00,5:17,13:59, 14:39. I hope you can check the video out for yourself.

I guess we can only view stars from here on the ground, since No stars are ever seen in the video.

In closing for this chapter, I would like to cover satellites briefly.

NASA's website says that "satellites orbits Earth when its speed is balanced by the pull of Earth's gravity."

One rather dubious fact stated by NASA is that the earth is surrounded by 13,000 satellites.

When one satellite malfunctions, NASA expect you to believe that the space shuttle has gone up with a crew to fix it.

Amazing task in itself to circumnavigate the sea of satellites that are traveling at 17,000 miles per hour.

If you asked me "Are Satellites real?" I will say a resounding NO! If they were real, one of these satellites would have already taken a real picture of another real satellite and of the earth that we live in.

However, NASA says that there are satellites that orbit east and west and appear to be stationary and are called geostationary satellites. Moreover, some satellites point down towards earth to observe wildfires, volcanos and other stuff. Why can't they do the simple task of taking a real picture of Earth?

Satellites are said to be orbiting anywhere between 1240 miles, which is Geocentric orbits. Then you have the Medium Earth Orbit satellites ranging in altitude between 1240 miles to 22,236 miles.

Are you serious? What technology do we have that would enable our astronauts to go up that high?

The highest the astronauts have ever gone was 400 miles and the dangerous electrons from the Van Allen radiation belt penetrated the space shuttle. Then the radiation penetrated their space suits and finally penetrated the pupils of their shut eyes. In 1994 CNN reported: "The radiation belts surrounding the Earth may be more dangerous for astronauts than previously believed. The phenomenon known as the 'Van Allen Belts' can spawn (newly discovered) 'Killer Electrons' that can dramatically affect the astronaut's health." Jonathan Mark wrote this in *Moon Landing Hoax*.

Moreover, satellites did not exist until a British Science fiction writer by the name of Sir Arthur Charles Clarke, a Freemason, wrote about them in one of his writings in a proposed satellite communication system in 1945. (Wikipedia fact).

But, I know what about Satellite dish right?

Well if they are tracking these hypothetical satellites, then the dish receiver that is mounted outside people's homes should be constantly moving, nonstop, since it would be tracking a satellite or two or three like they say, right?

Most of the pictures that I have ever seen that depicts a satellite in space is CGI. Once again, why can't NASA just get an astronaut that is in the ISS to get a video camera, and pan 360 degrees with his camera, and show us a satellite, and the earth, and according to the European Space Agency, the 6300 tons of space debris? According to Lucky Tran's article "Experience Just How Much Space Junk is Floating Around, in One Astounding Interactive," "the debris has a total mass of more than 6300 tons and can travel as fast as 35,000 miles per hour."

Please! Shut the front door....just in case the debris makes it to Earth.

I know what you may be thinking, to challenge my belief in real satellites in space.

How does GPS work, cell phones or the internet without satellites?

Well GPS uses trilateration which is the same thing as land based triangulation but it uses satellites instead. However, if you suspend your belief in satellites for just one minute let me propose an idea.

When a plane or ISS or space shuttle or even the Orion space craft goes over the Indian Ocean all coordinates or GPS signal is lost. Why do you suppose this happens?

The reason is that it is such an immense ocean that no towers were ever installed to truly be able to triangulate position of an object, say for example a ship or an airplane.

Why else do you see towers every 40 miles or so on land? The truth will astonish you.

The internet is actually buried cables in the ocean that carry all the data that we transmit across the World Wide Web.

Wikipedia states that "A submarine communications cable is a cable laid on the sea bed between land-based stations to carry telecommunication signals across stretches of ocean. The first submarine communications cables, laid in the 1850s, carried telegraphy traffic. Subsequent generations of cables carried telephone traffic, then data communications traffic. Modern cables use optical fiber technology to carry digital data, which includes telephone, internet and private data traffic."

Now you tell me, why, do we need imaginary satellites doing the same thing that these cables in the ocean are doing?

Once you accept the reality that NASA hoaxed the moon landing, coupled with the fact that the firmament is up there in space, believing in satellites is a conundrum.

I have not done a very thorough job in this chapter explaining all the evidence of the "Illusions and Hoaxes" employed by NASA, due to the limitation of the word count that I was aspiring for in writing my first book.

But, I do plan to continue my research, and hopefully find definitive proof down the road about the different space objects that we are told are up there in orbit around the Earth. It usually goes like this, an object is placed in orbit and then that's it, apparently, it magically sustains itself and avoids the other 2200 satellites and space junk. Furthermore, the metal that they are made out of must be from the Planet Krypton, since it doesn't melt.

In an article by Wild Heretic, entitled "Space machines do not orbit the Earth" he says that the temperature shoots up hotter the higher an object goes depending on sun activity. Wild Heretic says the following:

"As you can see, all three object [ISS, satellites, and Hubble telescope] above are in the seriously ferocious hot zone. Apart from nothing working at the minimum 600 degrees Celsius [or 1112 degrees Fahrenheit] due to thermal expansion of the materials (iron glows red hot at 500 degrees Celsius) some of the electronic components like lead, zinc, and epoxy resin would not just burn out, but melt."

Part II

EXPERIMENTS AND EVIDENCE OF A FLAT EARTH

We finally get to the last chapter of the book, and I call it "Evidence and Experiments."

I hope that by now, I have kept my promise of stimulating the neurons in your brain and made you think, and challenged your world view.

I am including experiments that have been conducted over the years to prove that the earth is flat.

Firstly, I would like to discuss the formula to calculate the curvature of the earth.

The formula states that the earth curves about 8 inches per mile squared. This is due to the earth's curvature which has a radius of about 3965 miles. The circumference, in case you don't know is 2 x 3.14 x radius. Which this would give us 6.28 x 3965 = 24,900 miles.

An easy example that I use to calculate the curvature of the earth is the following: Take an object that is 6 miles away from your location, then take 6 and square it and you get 36. Then take 36 miles and multiply by 8 inches and you get 288 inches. Divide 288 inches by 12 inches to get distance in feet and you get 24 feet. In other words, the object at the other end should be 24 feet below the horizon from two objects that are 6 miles apart from each other. Therefore, you should not be able to see that object any more due to the curvature of the earth and if the object is 24 feet below the horizon.

However, if you take some binoculars to look towards the same object towards the horizon, you will see that object that is 6 miles away in perfect view. Where the heck is the curvature? Or did the binoculars follow the curve of the earth?

So to get mathematical here, the curvature varies inversely as the square of the distance. In 3 miles, for example there is a decline of about 6 feet. i.e. 3 x 3 = 9 x 8 in = 72 / 12 = 6 ft.

So how can the following distance be explained when

people have seen the Chicago skyline which is 59 miles from the opposite shore of Lake Michigan?

Given the earth's curvature, it should be 2320 feet below the horizon. However, the Chicago sky line can be seen on a clear day. Meteorologists have chalked it up to it being a mirage. But the image is not inverted which would explain a mirage being refracted off the water of the lake. In this example, it is clear to see that the earth is a flat plane. Mr. Rob Skiba, recently debunked this as being a mirage when he went to the lake and recorded on camera the visible Chicago skyline from 30 miles away, if I remember correctly. You can find his video on YouTube.

In the old days, people used to explain a ship disappearing into the horizon due to the earth being a globe and curving downward into the horizon. This was the first proof that made people believe that earth had a curvature. However, all you need is a pair of binoculars and you will see the object that disappeared in the horizon since from your perspective the human eyes can see about 3 miles distance without binoculars. However, the higher in elevation that you go the farther you can see off into the horizon, on this flat earth that we live on.

Throughout my book, I have included research, observations, articles, and video information and websites from many knowledgeable experts debunking that the earth is a globe.

There have not been any experiments that can be replicated or conducted that proves that the earth is spinning around at 1048 mph at the equator and that we are revolving around the sun.

I'd like to say here, No Curvature, No Ape-Man, Know the Flat Earth!

I will take credit for a few things, as the originator, as far as I know.

I want to include the following: the term Masonic Induced Coma or Hypnosis, the observation about tubular design of the ISS to make it easier to fake on an airplane like a Boeing 747 or the like, the GPS position and coming back later to same coordinates. One more that I would like to add as the originator, as far as I know. I was watching a documentary once on Discovery Channel or History Channel. It discussed about sharks and whales migrating from the Atlantic Ocean all the way down to Costa Rica, and the experts were able to track their movements.

What I want to propose is, how can a shark or whale be able to find its bearings in the vast ocean if the earth is constantly rotating on its axis? The sharks must truly be an anomaly if they are able to do this without ending up somewhere else. However, these sea creatures do it every year, if I remember correctly, and they always find the same waters that they set out to find.

I am puzzled with GPS coordinates remaining the same. In other words, on any given day of the week, pick up your phone and get your GPS coordinates and record your location. You will get a latitude and longitude correct?

Ok, now wait a few days and return to the same location. Pull out your Garmin or your GPS phone and get the coordinates. Guess what? The longitude and latitude are the exact same coordinates, within a few inches of where you were the first time you inquired for coordinates. This is a true conundrum since it is very unlikely that if the earth moved 24,000 miles in 24 hours plus the amount of days that passed since you last returned to that spot, that the coordinates would be the same. I would think that the coordinates should change!!!

If its hard evidence that you need to persuade you then you came to the right place.

I want to include the rockets that have been launched into space with cameras that blow the globe theory out of the water!

In 1946 a V2 rocket that the U.S. confiscated from the Russians was launched into space with a camera. You have to watch this video. The rocket was launched from the U.S. Army's White Sands Missile Range in New Mexico on October 24, 1946.

On www.universetoday.com *"This is the Very First Photo of Earth from Space"* is the name of the video. The commentator states that a spectator on board the rocket could have seen San Diego, Salt Lake City, and San Antonio. Okay, let's stop here and let me calculate the distance of each of these cities from White Sands, NM.

From White Sands, NM to San Diego it is 624.25 miles away.

From White Sands, NM to Salt Lake City Utah it is 652.24 miles.

From White Sands, NM to San Antonio Texas it is 622 miles by road.

How can we see 720 miles off to the horizon and be able to see these cities?

Do you remember in the chapter where we figured the explanation of why at the top of the tallest building in Dubai the people could still see the Sun 2 minutes longer than the people at the bottom? This is only possible on a flat plane, which the Earth has to be!

According to the curvature of the Earth formula, they would be way down at least 50 miles beneath the horizon for any of these cities from the vantage point of the rocket camera to the horizon.

If you analyze the video frame by frame you will see the perfect flat horizon of the earth from 65 miles up in the sky, however, the commentator says that you can clearly see the curvature of the earth.

Maybe he needs glasses.

Kudos to the work of Missile Range engineer Clyde Holliday whose idea it was to mount the 35 mm camera on the V-2 rocket.

In the official report conducted they used words like "stationary flat plane", in referring to the earth.

However, the military chose to conceal this from the public and once again use the controlled media propaganda to state that the earth's was a globe with a curve.

In the following observation I want to challenge all non-believers of the Flat Earth!

I want to use the following rocket launch as my trump all, "Ace in the Hole," about debunking the heliocentric model and globe earth.

I am referring to the rocket launch by an independent 3rd party, the GoFast rocket and they set a record for the highest altitude launch by amateurs.

Please watch this video posted by Ky Michaelson, and it is called "GoFast 2014 HD OnBoard Cameras.

Or also the main video of the launch of the rocket is called "VNR CSXT GO FAST! Rocket Launch 2014 plus B roll High Res." You can find it on YouTube and it was posted by GoFastDrink.

The third video of the record obtained is posted by Bernie V Films.

"2014 Rocket Recovered!!! CSXT/ Go Fast Sports / Jet Pack Int'l." I believe that this video was posted by the main person in charge of the launch and the designer of the rocket that they used.

I really want to state a real and conclusive fact about the earth not being a globe.

If you pause the video once the rocket reaches space, you will see a flat horizon. In addition, what I want to stress here is that the Moon is clearly visible in the video. Some people say you can actually even see the ice wall that surrounds the flat earth. I can see it, but of course I am biased, so that doesn't count.

What matters to me is the fact that you can see the moon. Why is this important? Well, people in Australia stated that they could see the moon at that time in the blog from the after party "attaboys."

I got this idea from Peter Pan, on a YouTube video except he didn't find the exact time of the launch, and I did.

Once I obtained this information, I went to a website where you can actually track the location of the moon around the earth for any date and time.

It is www.timeanddate.com.

When I typed the date of the rocket launch which was July 14, 2014. Guess what it showed me?

It showed me that the moon was over Australia at the time of the rocket launch. Here is the picture for a visual aid.

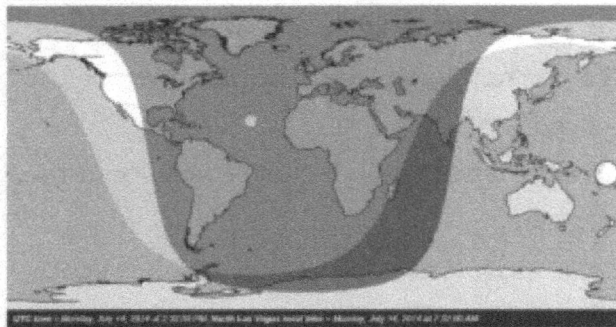

Moon Light World Map

In this picture, you can see that the moon is clearly above Australia. The video indicated that the rocket launched somewhere north of Nevada in a place called Black Rock Desert. It is 540 miles north of Las Vegas, Nevada.

In the Globe earth model, Australia is on the opposite side of the United States of America which is on the North American continent.

AUSTRALIA ON THE GLOBE

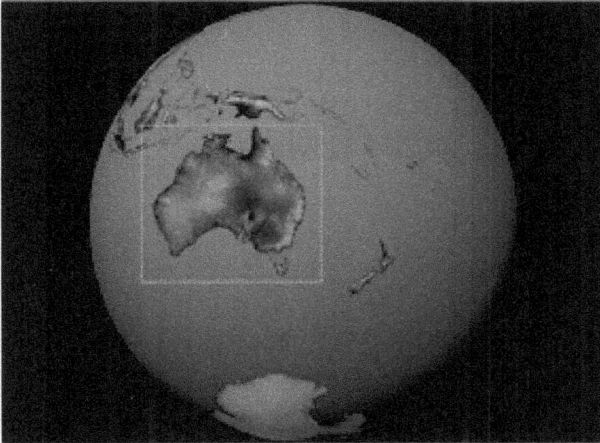

If the moon, which is shown in the above picture is on the right hand corner by Australia, how can the rocket that reached an amateur record distance of 73.1 miles, capture the Moon in the video, if the earth is a Globe?

Where is the curvature of the earth? I know it should be impossible to have captured the view of the moon, since the distance between Australia and Nevada is some 7300 miles. Clearly, in the Heliocentric Model of earth, if the moon is orbiting over Australia, then the rocket should not have captured the moon in the video.

AUSTRALIA ON THE GLOBE

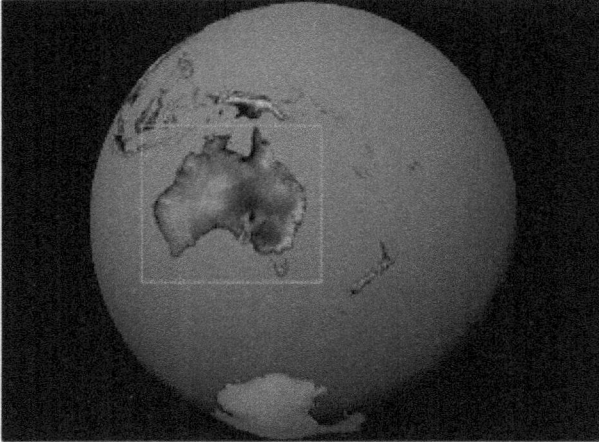

A projection of Australia as seen from space. Asia is to the north. The fake Antarctica continent is to the south. To the east is New Zealand. Africa to the west is out of view.

Clearly, you cannot see North America from Australia!!!!!

Here is the North American Continent and I am sure you can find Nevada on there. You can start to see the top of South America. On a globe earth, Australia is on the bottom opposite side of the Earth.

Just to reiterate, the video clearly showed the moon in space, yet the rocket was launched in Nevada.

If the Earth is a globe, then there is no way on God's green earth, that the rocket should have captured the moon when it went up 72 miles into space. By the way if the moon really is only 100 miles above our heads, then the video really shows the rocket almost at the same height as the moon.

I don't care if it went up 200 miles up, the Moon should not have been captured in this video.

One of my close friends, recently argued that since the Moon is 238,000 miles away if the rocket went up higher that the moon should be able to be seen. I don't think so buddy since the Earth is 4 times bigger than the Moon according to NASA. The other continents and ocean and land mass would prevent the rocket's camera from capturing a glimpse of the moon if the earth were a spinning ball.

The earth is actually way bigger, since the Moon is about 32 miles across according to the Flat Earth research.

However, **since the Earth is indeed flat,** then yes the Moon should be visible since it is a big enough object in the sky.

Remember in Revelation 1:7 "Look, he is coming with the clouds, and every eye will see him, even those who pierced him."

The only way that "every eye" will see God, is if the earth is a flat plane.

I got the official time of the launch of the rocket from the website www.rocketryforum.com. In an article entitled "*CSXT Space Shot 2014 10th Anniversary Flight.*" It reads "Today the CSXT team celebrated its 10 year anniversary of its first historic flight into space by launching another go Fast CSXT rocket into space. The flight took off at 7:32 AM Pacific time. The flawless flight was observed by the FAA, specific details will be posted later on."

There is an experiment that I want to conduct with the Globe Earth that I have in my room. What I want to do is insert 2 cameras into the globe and secure them down, so they don't move. One camera will be placed right above Australia and point straight up, and the other camera will be near the desert where the rocket was launched, (if I can find it on the globe) or somewhere in North Nevada. Then I will buy or build a fake miniature moon and I will ensure that it is about one fourth the size of the earth globe, since the moon is ¼ size of the earth. I will then bring the moon above Australia and activate both cameras and I want to see if the moon is visible from both the cameras by Australia and the camera by Nevada, or if it is only visible by the camera above Australia. This will replicate the Go Rocket video footage.

One last experiment that I think is worth mentioning in my book involved an experiment with a telescope. It is called "Airy's Failure" but is invaluable in proving a Geocentric Earth model.

In other words, George Airy was actually trying to prove that the earth moves but inadvertently proved the opposite, and hence the term "Airy's Failure" experiment.

Eric Dubay, once again, in "200 *Proofs Earth is Not a Spinning Ball*,"explains the following about the experiment:

The experiment knows as "Airy's Failure" proved that the stars move relative to a stationary Earth and not the other way around. By first filling a telescope with water to slow down the speed of light inside, then calculating the tilt necessary to the starlight directly down the tube [of the telescope] Airy failed to prove the heliocentric theory since the starlight was already coming in the correct angle with no change necessary, and instead proved the geocentric model correct," says Eric Dubay, in "200 Proofs that the Earth is Not a Spinning Ball."

Quoting from the same article about another experiment, "The Michelson-Morley and Sagnac experiments attempted to measure the change in speed of light due to Earth's assumed motion through space. After measuring in every possible direction in various locations they failed to detect any significant change whatsoever, again proving the stationary geocentric model."

I was talking to a friend of mine about my book and he started arguing and asking me questions trying to debunk the flat earth. However, once I mentioned about the position of Polaris over the North Pole never changing he changed his conviction.

In other words, if NASA says that the earth is rotating at 1000 mph and 24,000 miles in one day. Meanwhile, we are rotating around the sun at 67,000 mph. On top of that the sun itself, with the earth and all planets in tow, is rotating around the Milky Way. Why does Polaris never change its position in the night sky?

Polaris, according to NASA is in line with the imaginary tilt of the earth.

NASA actually says that before Polaris the North Star was a different star, but it changed to Polaris. It will change in another 21,000 years or so, and we will have a different North Star.

I am trying to wrap my brain around this concept as to how the North Star is maintaining its position in the Cosmos with all the planets including the earth traveling through space.

Sounds crazy to me, but it comes from NASA, so it must be true. Right?

One other important fact that I forgot to mention is the creation of NASA. It is a bit dark, but may be worth mentioning. Please do not judge an entire race of people by the atrocities of a few!

Norman in "The First Published Photographs of the Earth Taken from Space, he states that "As part of Project Paperclip, the United States government brought both the captured V-2's and over 100 German rocketry experts (headed by Werner von Braun) to America, where they began what became the U.S. space program."

In *Behind the secret plan to bring Nazi scientist to US*," Maureen Callahan says that "The legacy of Paperclip, Jacobsen writes, speaks to the triumph of pragmatism and self-interest above unthinkable atrocity." Callahan is referring to a book written by Annie Jacobsen called *"Operation Paperclip: The Secret Intelligence Program to Bring Nazi Scientists to America."*

Jacobsen shocked me with the revelation of the following Nazi actions:

"Simultaneously, the US government was learning

more and more about just what the Nazis had done: the extermination of millions of Jews; the mass sterilization, the live experiments and operations conducted without anesthesia on humans code-named 'adult pigs,' the systematic yanking of gold teeth, the slave labor and starvation, the drowning of men in ice-cold tubs and the many failed attempts to resurrect them, the exploding bodies forced into high-altitude chambers in efforts to master space flight."

To know that some of these Third Reich Nazis eventually became major NASA officials is gut wrenching to say the least.

I would like to close my book by giving you some final information as to the distance and size of the moon and the sun and the earth. As I understand it, from a Flat Earth Perspective.

The moon and the sun are 3000 miles away from the earth. In addition, the sun and the moon are about the same size, 32 miles across. The sun is one of the "great light" from scripture and so is the moon. The sun is not a nuclear furnace that burns hydrogen and helium with nuclear reactions and it is not 400 times the size of the moon or 400 times farther away, which is why NASA says they are the same size. In addition, the sun is not 98 million miles away from the earth. How do explain sun spots in clouds and in lakes. Or why do sun rays disperse into different angles in clouds if the sun were so far away, the sun beams should be going in one and the same direction.

I would like to add an experiment that I did using an infrared temperature gun. I shot the gun towards the sun and got a reading of 734 degrees Fahrenheit. and then I shot the moon and it was -4 degress Fahrenheit. I do not know what is going on here, however, I do believe that these two great light from scripture are closer than what we've been told by NASA.

According to Eric Dubay, the moon is not terra firma. In other words, no one can go up to it and land or drive a 4 wheeler like NASA showed, much less walk on it.

Why do you think we only see one side of the moon and can never see the dark side of the moon?

Antarctica encircles the entire earth, and so there is no southern hemisphere. According to my research "The great Ice Wall" which is what encircles the entire Earth, should be reached, if a person heads straight south at a latitude of about 78 degrees south latitude from any location.

Polaris is always Earth's center and it is directly above the North Pole.

The equator is a circle half way between the North Pole and the South Ice Wall.

We can circumnavigate the earth from east to west or vice versa. However, no one can circumnavigate the earth from north to south, for as David Wardlaw Scott, in Terra Firma puts it, "we cannot break through intervening lands, nor pass the impenetrable ramparts of ice and rocks which enclose the great Southern Circumference."

The Moon is a self-luminating translucent disk. In other words, it does not reflect sunlight. For example, "the sun's light is golden, warm, drying, preservative and antiseptic, while the Moon's light is silver, cool, damp, putrefying and septic. The Sun's rays decrease the combustion of a bonfire, while the Moon's rays increase combustion. On a clear night, during a waxing or waning cycle, it is even possible to occasionally see stars and planets directly through the surface of the Moon!" This all according to aplanetruth in "Stars Through a Translucent Moon You Can See for Yourself."

One last fact, really quickly, there is a Flat Earth Society, that is actually run by Freemasons, or some other third party that wants to sabotage the great progress that the true Flat Earth researchers, are trying to accomplish.

Please be aware of this!

Also, watch out for what we call "Trolls" and they are people that go to flat earth forums and always are quick to hate and spread lies about the spinning ball earth.

Even rapper B.o.B a.k.a. Bobby Ray Simmons, recently pissed off NASA's poster boy and spokesman, Neil Degrasse Tyson when he released a CD that has a logo of the Flat Earth, and I think he even has a rap about the flat earth.

Low and behold, who comes to the Freemason's rescue? Yup, Neil Degrasse Tyson, and he hires his nephew, who is studying poetry or something in college, to come back with a rap of his own, and then Neil Degrasse

Tyson, drops the mic at the end of his performance on some talk show, as if to show that he won the battle.

Do you see why they are nervous, and paranoid?

I really think, it's because of the Flat Earth truth, coupled with the realization that God's warriors are gaining momentum, with our strength in numbers.

In the last couple of years the Flat Earth movement, has become a formidable group of individuals that are trying to expose the truth of the real world that we live.

I would love to keep going and going, like the Energizer bunny on here, but I set a goal for myself of writing a book of about 28,000 words and I seemed to have reached my goal, and then some.

I do hope that I was able to challenge your belief system about what you have been indoctrinated to believe. I am sure you can agree that "The Captivated Audience: Hoaxes, Illusions and the Biblical Earth," that we live in deserves more investigation and prudence in navigating the waters of research and enlightenment. Please be cognizant of the indoctrination that we've been taught. Only you can decide when enough deception and lies is enough.

I hope that you are in accordance with me when I say that pseudo-science is a slippery slope. One theory begat another and another and there is no end in sight. They have to continuously invent or fabricate CGI images to convince the masses of the fake spinning ball earth universe that man created.

"It's easier to fool people than to convince them that they've already been fooled."

– Mark Twain

We are all interconnected in some way, shape, or form. After all, technology brings us all closer together. Please be aware of the propaganda that exists in music, movies, books, newspapers, magazines, internet, that will continue to make you believe that the earth is an oblate spheroid that spins.

Please continue to read and to learn more and snap out of the "Masonic Induced Hypnosis" then, you too will no longer be an unknowing and unassuming member of the "Captivated Audience", but instead you will be an "awakened" God loving, and pragmatic individual.

I would like to take the time to thank you for buying my book.

2 Corinthians 13:14 (ESV)

"The grace of the Lord Jesus Christ, and the love of God and the fellowship of the Holy Spirit be with you all."

THE END

www.ingramcontent.com/pod-product-compliance
Lightning Source LLC
LaVergne TN
LVHW011912080426
835508LV00007BA/489